Haynes
Computer
Manual

© Haynes Publishing 2002

First published 2001
Revised 2nd edition 2002

Published by: Haynes Publishing
Sparkford, Yeovil, Somerset BA22 7JJ
Tel: 01063 442030 Fax: 01963 440001
Int. tel: +44 1963 442030 Fax: +44 1963 440001
E-mail: sales@haynes-manuals.co.uk
Web site: www.haynes.co.uk

British Library Cataloguing in Publication Data:
A catalogue record for this book is available from the British Library

ISBN 1 85960 888 4

Printed in Britain by J. H. Haynes & Co. Ltd., Sparkford

Haynes

Computer
Manual

The step-by-step guide to upgrading, repairing and
maintaining a PC

Haynes Publishing

COMPUTER MANUAL
Contents

Introduction

Let's begin by asking two questions. Do you consider your home desktop computer system to be a fabulously powerful, immensely flexible, wholly essential and user-friendly tool? Or do you regard it as an overly complex, befuddling contraption, riddled with conflicting standards, prone to break down in any number of bizarre ways, instantly obsolete and bedevilled with an incomprehensible jargon developed by, and for, fully-fledged geeks?

Your answer to both questions is probably 'yes'. That's where we come in.

If you enjoy using your computer and want to make the most of your hardware (and your money) without becoming a dyed-in-the-wool techie in the process, this is the book for you. We'll show you in a series of clear step-by-step guides just how to upgrade, improve and enhance your system. We'll also consider how best to trouble-shoot problems and keep it all running smoothly. Above all, we'll endeavour to make everything easy.

Do please remember one thing: a computer is not like this year's model of a particular make of car. It's simply not possible for us to predict with any degree of certainty what's sitting on your desktop. Quite the reverse, in fact. The very essence and, indeed, appeal of the personal computer is that one size resolutely does not suit all: you can make of your system just what you will. This inevitably means that there are limitations to what we can cover here, and so our approach throughout is to focus on the most likely and common configurations.

The alternative – and there is only one – is to try to cover all angles, all bases, all permutations, all possible problems. What you end up with then is a massively unwieldy tome that ties itself in knots with cross-references and tables and endless ifs and buts … and still doesn't succeed in its aims.

No, we've striven instead to cover the basics and to give you enough background knowledge to tackle your own computer setup with confidence.

To that end, we're making certain assumptions here.

First, about you:

You have a working (although not necessarily thorough) knowledge of Windows

You don't have an unlimited budget (or else you'd buy a brand new computer every 6 months and stay ahead of the game)

You're not scared to perform minor surgery on your computer (but you'd rather know what you're doing than fumble in the dark)

And secondly, about your computer:

It has a Pentium processor or equivalent (definitely not an old 486, but probably not a shiny Pentium 4 either)

It's running Windows 95, 98 or Millennium Edition (not Windows 3.1)

It dates back no further than 1994/5

It has an internet connection (not essential but very, very helpful)

It's a PC, not a Mac!

Just a word on that last comment. Mac users are a sorely overlooked species in much computer literature. True, there aren't that many of them around, relatively speaking, despite the popular iMac, but that's no excuse. The real point is that a Mac has quite a different architecture to a PC and a significantly different operating system, and it's simply impractical, unhelpful and ultimately unfair to stick in the odd 'oh, and if you have a Mac, you might want to try this…' section in a book that deals primarily with PCs. That is why we wrote a separate manual specifically for Mac users, entitled *The Haynes Mac Manual*.

This, then, is the manual for the discerning but probably somewhat frustrated owner of an 'average' Windows-based Pentium-powered PC. We can't promise to turn it into a supercomputer overnight but we certainly hope to help you prolong its lifespan and/or make it significantly better.

We keep the jargon to a minimum and practical guidance to the fore. After all, reading about computers is probably not high on your list of priorities, and upgrading, repairing and maintaining your hardware is not, with the best will in the world, what you might call fun. But using your computer should be fun and that's the point of this manual: to help ensure that your PC serves you well both now and in the future, however your needs may change.

1

PART **1** Getting to know your PC

First things first. Before we start poking around under the hood, let's take stock of your current computer setup. We're not exactly doing rocket science here but the best place to start is undoubtedly with a little basic background knowledge.

GETTING TO KNOW YOUR PC

A brief history of personal computing

It has become something of a cliché to say that the Apollo moon missions were managed with less computing power than you'll find in today's typical car, electronic organiser, digital watch or musical greetings card... but it illustrates the pace of progress well. These days, everything from your kettle to your keyring carries a microchip and that bland, beige box perched on your desktop is capable of performing more calculations in a split second than any mere mortal could achieve in a hundred lifetimes.

But it's a mistake to allow yourself to be overawed by technology. Always remember that a computer is a tool – no more and no less. It may be faster but you're smarter. (No, honestly, you are.) The chances are that you'll never *really* understand how your computer works, but so what? What counts is understanding how all the various bits and pieces work *together*. Grasp that and you'll soon be stripping, upgrading and rebuilding your PC before breakfast.

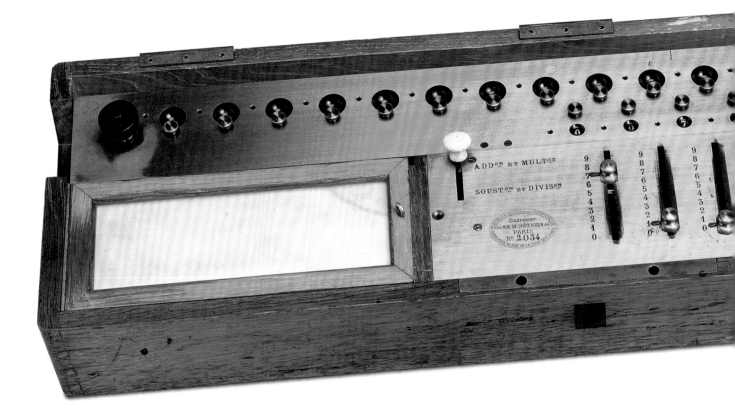

A functioning computer is essentially comprised of three parts

Hardware: *the motherboard, memory, processor, monitor, keyboard, modem, mouse and all the other nuts and bolts stuff.*

Operating system: *the master program that makes the hardware and software work together in perfect harmony (usually).*

Application software: *programs that let you do useful things with your PC like write letters, perform calculations, surf the internet and much, much more.*

Charles X Thomas de Colmar invented his Arithmometer in 1820. It was the first commercially successful calculating machine and could be used for addition, subtraction, division and multiplication.

If you can get the distinction between hardware, the operating system and application software clear in your mind from the outset, then you've overcome one major hurdle. But if, for now, you don't know Windows from Word, ROM from RAM or a chipset from a chipolata, don't panic! You will, we promise.

So just how did we get here? Well, ask any two specialists about what really matters in the story of computing and you'll likely get two very different answers. But the one thing that they – and we – will agree upon is this: despite the chequered, convoluted and complex evolution of the personal computer, these days just about *anybody* can get to grips with the technology. What was once the exclusive province of boffins is now familiar territory to millions.

And that's a good thing. All you need is a little patience, a dash of logic, the confidence to tinker – and, of course, this manual as your guide.

A Chinese Abacus, the Suan Pan is the oldest form of abacus still in use.

Charles Babbage's Difference engine was finished in 1822. It was a decimal digital machine.

A controversial timeline

500BC Ernie the Egyptian invents the abacus. Blame him

1642 Blaise Pascal invents an automatic adding machine of sorts

1674 Gottfried von Leibniz upgrades the Pascaline by adding multiplication

1822 Charles Babbage designs his Difference Engine, a mechanical calculator, but can't raise sufficient venture capital to build it

1833 Babbage upgrades his earlier invention to an Analytical Engine but doesn't build this one either

1890 Herman Hollerith comes up with a method for using punched cards to store data

1911 The Computing-Tabulating-Recording Company is founded in New York, and soon becomes IBM (International Business Machines)

1939 John Vincent Atanasoff and Clifford Berry invent the first true digital computer

1943 Alan Turing invents the *other* first true digital computer, Colossus, and uses it to crack the Germans' wartime Enigma code

1946 John Presper Eckert and John Mauchly develop ENIAC (Electronic Numerical Integrator And Computer), a fully-fledged computer replete with processor. It weighed in at 30 tonnes

1951 Eckert and Mauchly unveil UNIVAC (Universal Automatic Computer), the first computer to be sold commercially on the high street. It cost around $5m

1958 IBM develops a computer that uses transistors instead of valves

1964 The integrated circuit is used for the first time in computer design

1965 Digital Equipment Corporation launches the first minicomputer, the PDP-8

1969 The US Department of Defense sets up a computer network called ARPANet (Advanced Research Projects Agency) that will one day become the internet

1970 The UNIX operating system is developed. So is the 8 inch floppy disk

1973 The first hard disk arrives courtesy of IBM: a 30MB tiddler called Winchester

1975 The Altair 8800 – the first microcomputer, or PC – is sold to the public. It cost $400 and you had to build it yourself. Bill Gates and Paul Allen found Microsoft

The large disk is from an IBM system of 1984 and can hold 4MB, compared with the small hard disk from 1999 which can hold 6GB!

The Altair 8800b microcomputer of 1975.

'PalmPilot' palmtop computer of 1998. Manufactured by US Robotics.

1976 Steve Jobs and Steve Wozniak found Apple Computer

1978 The 5.25 inch floppy disk becomes the (temporary) standard medium for portable, removable storage

1980 British inventor Clive Sinclair launches the kit-form ZX-80 computer. Sales of soldering irons soar and a generation of geeks is born. It cost £79.95 plus £8.95 for the power supply. Ready-assembled model launched a month later at £99.95 to wicked and unsubstantiated rumours that they were customer-assembled models returned to Sinclair for repair

1981 The IBM PC hits the streets at £3000 and Acorn releases the popular BBC Micro. The 3.5 inch floppy disk also makes its first appearance

1982 The PC wins Time Magazine's 'Man of the Year' and the Sinclair ZX Spectrum brings computer games to the mass market

1984 Apple introduces the Macintosh computer. It uses a mouse and clickable icons and menus

1985 The first commercial version of Windows is launched by Microsoft

1988 Apple sues Microsoft for copying the graphical look and feel of its operating system. Then again, Apple allegedly pinched the idea from Xerox

1991 Tim Berners-Lee invents the World Wide Web. Life is never quite the same again

1994 Jeff Bozos quits Wall Street and decides to start an internet bookstore, Amazon.com

1995 Microsoft introduces Windows 95, which looks suspiciously like the Apple Mac. People suddenly find PCs easy to use, sales skyrocket, and Bill Gates becomes rather rich.

1996 Microsoft introduces Internet Explorer and sets off a browser war with Netscape, ultimately making web browsing software free.

1999 Internet businesses become the hottest stocks around the world. Millionaires are created as fast as you can say IPO

2000 The great dotcom crash! Reality kicks in and web businesses go to the wall in droves

2001 In the wake of the crash, PC and peripheral prices fall, making computer hardware the best buy ever

2002 Processors are now well into the 2 GHz-plus range i.e. capable of performing over two billion calculations per second. Ernie the Egyptian spins in his sarcophagus with the excitement of it all. Now let's get to work…

PART ① Why upgrade?

Back in 1965, a rising young engineer called Gordon Moore (who went on to co-found Intel) noted that computers had a habit of doubling in power every 18 months or so. His observation came to be enshrined as 'Moore's Law' and remarkably still holds true today. Ironically, we long ago passed the point where we actually *need* more computing power in our homes and offices, and yet still we rush lemming-like to upgrade or replace hardware that's barely out of warranty. Why?

Because I can? No, no, no... that's the answer of an inveterate geek. Now there's nothing wrong with being an inveterate geek – well, okay, there is, but we won't go into that here – but if you're the type to fix things that positively ain't broke, this ain't the book for you.

Because I want to? Really? You get kicks from tinkering with hardware? *Really?* There's certainly much satisfaction to be had from fixing or improving a PC but we'd draw the line at calling it fun.

Because I must? Absolutely. This is the only time when it makes true sense to upgrade your PC. There are, in fact, three quite distinct (good) reasons to upgrade:

Three good reasons to upgrade

To improve performance This is when your existing setup simply isn't up to the demands placed upon it, often as a result of changes in your own work or play habits. A system purchased to look after the accounts is unlikely to cut the mustard at 3-D gaming.

While performance-enhancing upgrades can significantly prolong the lifespan of your PC, it's important to make the *right* upgrades. As we go along, we'll consider which upgrades are practicable and worthwhile – and when it's better to admit defeat, throw the whole system in the skip and start afresh with a brand new computer!

To repair a broken component Unfortunately, unless you're a dab hand with a soldering iron, your chances of actually repairing anything are slim indeed. You *could* take a can opener to a stalled hard disk or hotwire a sound card... but we wouldn't advise it. No, the fact is that when something breaks down, it almost always need replacing – and in such cases it's easy to make a virtue of necessity by installing something altogether better. Why replace an ancient, slow CD-ROM drive with like for like when you could just as easily fit a shiny new CD-Recordable or Rewriteable drive instead, thereby simultaneously effecting a repair, boosting performance *and* adding new functionality?

To add new features Want to play DVD movies on your PC? Need a backup device? Run out of hard disk space? Fancy a bigger monitor or better printer? How about adding a hub to hook up two or more PCs in a home network? These are examples of upgrading a system by adding things that are currently lacking. Again, we'll look at all the options.

Boosting, repairing and enhancing a PC are all good reasons for minor surgery.

But before we get carried away, let's consider two further questions

Do you need really *need* to upgrade? Please understand that we're not trying to discourage you from upgrading your PC – quite the reverse – but there are times when a little sober reflection can pay dividends and save you money. For instance, is your software placing unnecessary demands on your hardware? Do you really need that full-blown, memory-hogging monolithic office suite just to balance the household budget? Would it be worthwhile buying a dedicated games console instead of converting your dusty old computer to a lean, mean fighting/driving/flying machine? Is your hard disk clogged with seldom-used programs that could be easily deleted to free up space? And would simply defragmenting your hard disk make a world of difference to your PC's performance?

If much of this sounds deeply mysterious right now, don't panic! We'll cover all the angles in detail soon enough. But if you're contemplating an upgrade simply because your once fleet of foot system is now limping lamely, jump straight to the Maintenance section on page 121. A little rudimentary house-keeping can work wonders – and save you a packet.

Can you upgrade? A recent trend in computer design has arguably made it easier to get up and running with a PC straight out of the box. But when integrated multimedia circuitry replaces fiddly expansion cards, it is tricky – if not impossible – to upgrade to a new graphics or sound card later. Similar thinking dictates that outmoded internal 'legacy' interfaces should be swept aside in favour of cheaper, more reliable machines that can be expanded indefinitely through USB and FireWire ports. Again, however, this renders many older but still serviceable peripherals instantly obsolete.

One day, perhaps, all PCs will be made this way. One day, perhaps, PCs will be ten a penny and it'll be cheaper to buy a new one that fuss around with upgrades and repairs. One day, perhaps, PCs will be genuinely easy to use. And one day, just perhaps, the PC will cease to exist in anything like its current shape and form.

But not today, and probably not tomorrow. For now, millions of us own computer systems that are teetering on the edge of obsolescence but not quite ready for the skip. This is the manual for people who can use a screwdriver but not a soldering iron; people who won't throw good money after bad but don't want to buy a new computer unless and until they absolutely have to; and people who are allergic to acronyms.

PART **1** **Outside explained**

DVD-ROM (Read-Only Memory) drive *Now commonplace, few older PCs have a DVD drive as standard. DVD drives read discs that look similar to CDs but have much more storage capacity. Application software is increasingly distributed in DVD format. DVD-ROM drives can also play movie discs.*

CD-ROM/R/RW drive *A compact disc player that handles multimedia CDs as well as the plain audio CD format. With most CD-ROM drives, a flat tray pops out and sucks the disk into the machine. CD-R (Recordable) and RW (Rewriteable) drives also let you make your own CDs using data on your computer, including music and video files.*

On/off switch *Does just what you'd expect. Of course, you know better than to switch off a PC without first going through the proper Windows shut down procedure, don't you (bizarre though it may be to press a Start button to stop the operating system)?*

Floppy drive *Floppy disks are a stalwart form of removable media. But while they may be cheap, the drives are sluggish and capacity is limited to 1.44MB per disk.*

Power LED *This light lets you know that your computer is switched on, just in case the fan wasn't loud enough to clue you in.*

Drive activity LED *A light that flashes when you read or write date from or to the hard disk.*

Reset switch *When Windows freezes and all else fails, this button restarts the system. Not one to push in error.*

Case *The majority of PCs now come in tower format (tall and narrow) rather than desktop (flat and wide). There are various standards governing case design, related to the size and shape of the motherboard within. If you were building a PC from scratch, this would be your first concern. See Appendix 5 on p159.*

Interface All this talk of ports and sockets and connectors may sound baffling – and let's be honest, you couldn't contrive to concoct a more counter-intuitive, jargon-riddled language if you tried – but keep in mind that these are just different types of interface. An interface, of course, is just a way of connecting two bits of kit and getting them talking to each other. It would be easier if everything used the *same* interface, but then you wouldn't need this manual. See p158 for a close-up guide to common connectors.

Power socket *A three-pin power cable plugs in here to connect your computer to the mains electricity.*

Power switch *If present (don't worry if it's not), this switch controls the internal power supply.*

PS/2-type ports *6-pin female sockets, one for the mouse and one for the keyboard. These are generally colour-coded green and purple respectively. Older systems may have a larger 5-pin round plug called a DIN socket for the keyboard, and sometimes the mouse has to use a serial port.*

USB ports *Newer sockets generally not found on PCs built before 1997/8. Faster and more flexible than either the parallel or serial port, USB (Universal Serial Bus) is becoming the de facto standard for connecting external devices.*

Audio connectors *A PC fitted with a sound card will typically have one or two outlets for speakers and jacks for connecting a microphone and other audio equipment. It may also have a game port designed for a joystick. This example is unusual because it features both built-in sound capabilities and a separate sound card. The built-in circuitry has been disabled to allow the more powerful sound card to run the show.*

Cooling fan *Air inlet for the internal fan. Without suitable cooling, a PC would soon get hot enough to fry an egg. And its own circuitry.*

Ethernet connector *If the PC has networking capabilities built in, there will be an 8-pin RJ-45 socket for connecting it to a hub or directly to another computer.*

Serial port *A 9-pin male socket commonly used to connect external modems and older mice. Two such ports are the norm, known to Windows as COM1 and COM2.*

Parallel port *A 25-pin female socket commonly used to connect a printer. Windows refers to this port as LPT1.*

Monitor connector *A 15-pin female socket used to connect the monitor. This is the visible end of the internal graphics card. Depending upon the capabilities of the card, there may also be an array of video outputs. Here we see an S-Video port for broadcasting a signal to a television set and also a digital connector for use with the very latest digital LCD monitors.*

Modem connector *If the PC has an internal modem, there will be a 6-pin RJ-11 socket to connect it to the telephone system via a cable.*

PART  **Inside explained**

We don't suggest for a minute that you dive straight to the innards of your PC but we're going to be talking a lot about motherboards, components and expansion cards as we go on. Here's a sneak preview of what to expect under the hood.

Power supply *A metal-cased assembly that converts AC power into the special low current voltages required by your computer.*

Processor *Usually thought of as the brains of a computer, the processor does number crunching on a grand scale. Chances are you'll have either an Intel or an AMD processor onboard, sitting either in a socket mounting (flat on the motherboard) or in a slot (on edge). The odds are it'll be hidden under a fan or a spiky metal heatsink to keep it cool.*

Graphics card *The graphics card is a printed circuit board responsible for producing the images that you see on your monitor screen. It's possible to build the circuitry right into the motherboard but this is an example of an expansion card (discussed in detail on p.74).*

Free expansion slots *These special spaces provide a place and socket for adding new capabilities to your computer*

Sound card *Another expansion card and, as you might expect, this one controls the PC's sound capability. Note the lead linking the sound card to the CD-ROM drive. This enables the card to pick up the soundtrack on an audio CD or CD-ROM and broadcast it through speakers or headphones.*

CD-ROM drive

Floppy drive

Hard disk *The hard disk is a device that permanently stores data until such time as you decide to delete or modify it. Every time you hit the Save button in a word processor, for instance, the document you're working on is copied to the hard disk, so it's safe even if the power is suddenly switched off. The process of saving data is called* writing *to the hard disk; retrieving it is* reading *from the hard disk.*

Memory *Random Access Memory, or RAM. It comes in sticks called memory modules and sits in rows on the motherboard. RAM is a temporary working space in which the PC's business is conducted from moment to moment.*

Motherboard *A great big printed circuit board. You really can't miss it because everything else plugs into it one way or another. Think of it as your PC's nervous system – a series of channels and conduits transmitting information from any one part of the system to any other. Getting hold of the manual that came with your motherboard is going to save a lot of headaches and uncertainty later.*

TECHIE CORNER

Drive Bays A drive bay is a socket in the case of a PC into which a drive may be installed. For reasons too dull to discuss, two sizes evolved, as shown here. Floppy and hard disk drives use the 3.5 inch standard, and virtually everything else the 5.25 inch standard. Note that the latter is also referred to as a half-height drive, so don't panic if you come across the term.

Drive bay	3.5"	5.25"
Actual width	4"	5.75"
Actual depth	5.75"	8"
Actual height	1"	1.63"

PART 1 **Peripherals explained**

The items on these pages are examples of what are commonly referred to as peripherals. You might be surprised to find the monitor comes under this heading – after all, you can't do much with a PC without one – but the hard disk is also, strictly speaking, a peripheral device. That is, a computer is still technically a computer without a storage device, a display unit or input devices. What it patently is not is useful! That's where peripherals come in: they let you do exciting, fun, useful stuff with your computer.

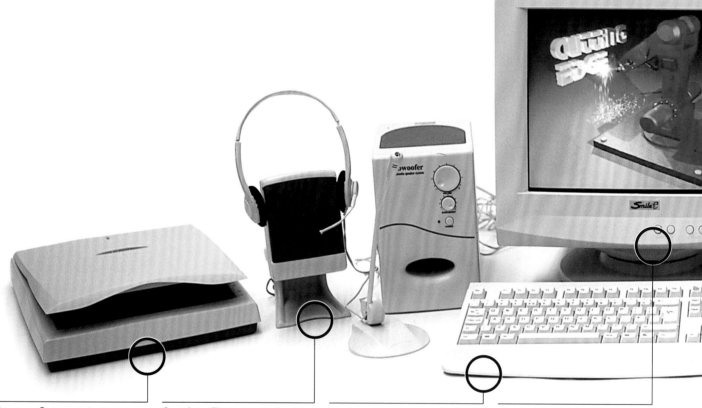

Scanner *Scanners turn documents and pictures into digital images which you can then view and play with on the PC. Strictly optional but rather useful.*

Speakers *These range from cheap, tinny and worthless to quite extraordinarily powerful. Speakers plug into the sound card.*

Keyboard *A dumb typewriter renowned for accumulating crumbs and other debris. It translates the motion of your fingers pressing keys into digital codes that your computer interprets as numbers, letters, and commands.*

Monitor *A display screen housed within a big, deep, bulky box – or, if it's modern, perhaps a smaller, flatter, less bulky box.*

Peripherals It's possible to add no end of peripheral devices to a computer. Indeed, it's this very expandability that makes the PC such a flexible tool. A webcam, for instance, lets you make face-to-face calls to family overseas; a graphics tablet turns a computer into a digital easel; and a MIDI keyboard opens up all manner of musical possibilities.

Webcam.

Graphics tablet.

MIDI keyboard.

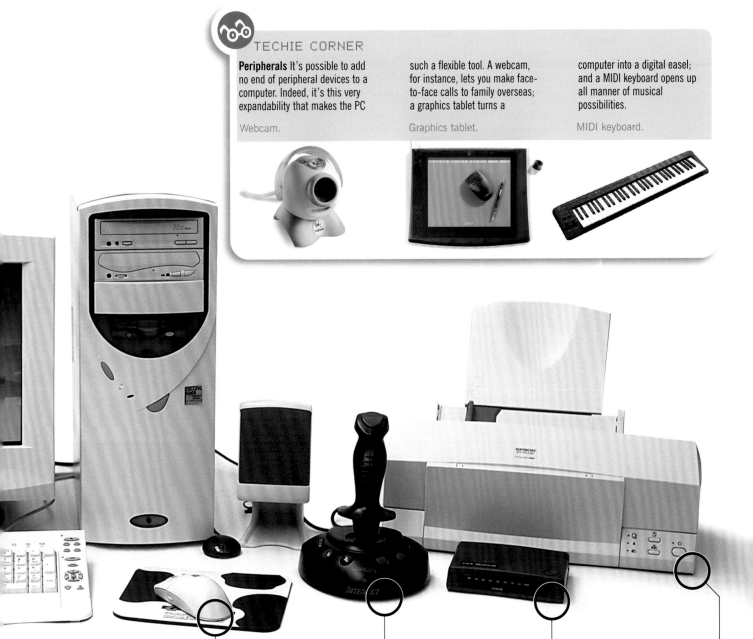

Mouse Small plastic clickable rodent that lives on a mat. The premiere pointing device, the mouse allows you to issue commands and move objects without typing.

Joystick Worthwhile to get the most out of computer games.

Modem Essential equipment for accessing the internet or sending paperless faxes. A modem translates computer data into sounds that can be sent down a standard phone line to other computers. Many PCs come with modems pre-installed internally on an expansion card, but stand-alone units are also available (and much easier to manage). A DSL router or cable modem serves the same purpose as the modem but provides higher speed – often called 'broadband' – access to the internet

Printer Despite the dream of a paperless office, hard copies of documents still have a place in most of our lives. The printer turns your computer's output into hard copy, nowadays with photo-like colour.

PART 1

GETTING TO KNOW YOUR PC

Taking stock

If you've ever bought off-the-shelf software, you'll know that there's usually a panel on the box stating the 'minimum system requirements'. Along the lines of:

IBM PC or 100% compatible computer
Intel Pentium 90MHz or higher processor
Windows 95, 98, Me, 2000, NT4 or XP
16MB of RAM (32MB recommended)
114MB free hard disk space
CD-ROM drive
Monitor 256-colour VGA or better
Sound card
Internet connection

But what does it all mean? And does your PC come up to scratch? That's one issue; another crops up when you come to go shopping for upgrade components. You see, you can't just go buy a bit more RAM without knowing what *kind* of RAM you need. And how much. And whether there's space for it on the motherboard.

The good news is if you start off with a thorough inventory of your current system, you really can't go far wrong. First of all, dig out the paperwork that came with your new PC. Here, you should find all the main specifications clearly laid out. However, that's only going to get you so far (and, of course, it's highly possible that you no longer have or simply can't find the original documentation). Thus we turn to Windows.

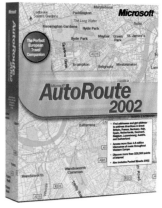

Check the minimum system requirements before you splash out on software.

Device advice

Click Start.
Click Settings.
Click Control Panel.

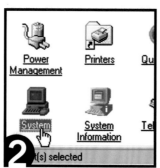

Click System.

Click the Device Manager tab. *Now, just by using Device Manager, you can investigate your entire hardware setup at a glance. Click the + sign alongside any component to see more detail. In this example, we've expanded the CD-ROM section and can see that there are two drives installed (one made by Mitsumi, the other by Samsung).*

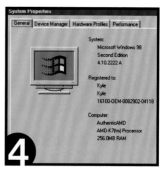

Next, *click the General tab to see how much RAM is inside your PC – in this case, 256MB. We can also see that the processor is an AMD model.*

Speed trap

Curiously, you won't find any mention of your processor's speed, although you should see it appear briefly if you watch the monitor screen carefully when you first start your PC. Not convinced? Then download and run the following utilities: For an Intel processor:

http://support.intel.com/support/processors/tools/frequencyid/download.htm
For an AMD processor: **http://www.amd.com/products/cpg/bin/cpuinfo.exe**

Unfortunately, and unhelpfully, the Intel version does not work with processors earlier than the Pentium III range. In this case, download the free version of Sandra (System ANalyser, Diagnostic and Reporting Assistant) and run the CPU & BIOS module: **http://www.sisoftware.co.uk/sandra**

In fact, Sandra's many tools will tell you just about everything you'll ever need to know about your system – hardware, software, technical configurations – and it's easier to use and clearer than Windows' own tools. The commercial version ($29 US at the time of writing) has 70 separate modules that between them cover every base.

Software utilities let you see just what your system is made of.

Rooting around

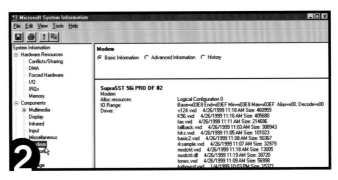

In Windows 98 and Millennium Edition, *another non-surgical route to the heart of your system is the System Information tool:*
Click Start.
Click Programs.
Click Accessories.
Click System Tools.
Click System Information.

Again, *click the + signs to see details of your system. Be sure to select the Basic Information option. Windows 95 users can also use System Information but it may look rather different to this picture.*

PART  **Taking precautions**

Before turning another page, and certainly before taking a screwdriver to your computer, ask yourself these questions:
How would I cope if my PC refuses to restart?
How would I cope if my files become corrupted?
How would I cope if my PC is stolen?
Temporary inconvenience or a major catastrophe? If your computer went badly awry, would you lose a day's work, a week's work, or the sum total of your efforts over the past year?

Safe or sorry?

It's important to recognise the difference between a computer failure and the loss of data. In the case of a software problem, it's usually possible to reinstall Windows (and any of your programs that you need to) from scratch. Tedious, but possible, and with luck all your documents and files will survive. However, a better idea is to take precautionary measures now, and that means making a startup disk. This way, you'll stand a good chance of fixing the problem from within. At the very least, you should be able to make emergency copies of your files.

Losing data is an altogether more serious proposition. No matter how careful you are, *any* computer upgrade, repair or maintenance carries with it a risk of damage. The only sensible approach – and believe us, we speak from hard and bitter experience – is to make backup copies of all your important files. In fact, make multiple copies, do it regularly, and keep them somewhere safe (and safe does not mean in your desk drawer: it means in an entirely different location, ideally in a fireproof box hidden under somebody else's floorboards!). There's a good chance that you made a Windows startup disk (or rescue, emergency or boot disk – they're all one and the same thing) when you first bought or acquired your computer. There's a higher chance still that you've since misplaced it, so let's make a fresh one now. Just follow these step-by-step instructions.

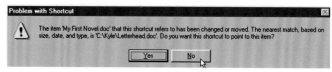

Lost files are at best a headache but can sometimes prove disastrous.

Making a Windows 98/Millennium Edition startup disk

First, *insert a blank floppy disk in its drive.*
Click Start.
Click Settings.
Click Control Panel.

Double-click *the Add/Remove Programs icon.*

Click *the Startup Disk tab.*

Click *Create Disk.*

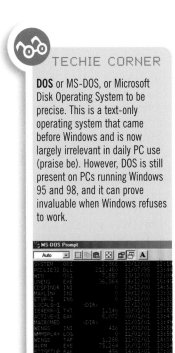

TECHIE CORNER

DOS or MS-DOS, or Microsoft Disk Operating System to be precise. This is a text-only operating system that came before Windows and is now largely irrelevant in daily PC use (praise be). However, DOS is still present on PCs running Windows 95 and 98, and it can prove invaluable when Windows refuses to work.

That's it. To test the disk, leave it in its drive and restart your PC. Instead of seeing the familiar Windows screen – remember, this is for emergencies when Windows itself is in need of repair – the computer will stay in DOS-mode and give you the option to start it up with or without CD-ROM support. Select the **with support** option. When you see a blinking **A:\>** prompt, type **D:** (assuming that D: is the drive letter usually assigned to your CD-ROM drive). Now put a disc in the CD-ROM drive, type **dir** and press the Enter key. If you can see a list of the files on the disk, congratulations. You could now reinstall Windows from the original CD-ROM (which you do, of course, still have safe, right?). In the meantime, remove the floppy disk from its drive, label it Windows Startup Disk, and press the reset switch. Windows will now start as normal.

Making a Windows 95 startup disk

Oh dear. It all gets a bit messy now. The problem is that Windows 95 startup disks do not include drivers for the CD-ROM drive. In other words, although the disk will start the system and allow you to carry out rudimentary repair work (if you know how), there's no way to access the CD-ROM drive. What *this* means is that you can't reinstall Windows because that requires access to, er, the CD-ROM drive. Not brilliant, is it?

The solution is to locate a DOS driver for your CD-ROM drive and include it on the startup disk. If you're lucky, and if you've kept everything that shipped with the original equipment, you may find a floppy disk helpfully labelled 'this is a DOS driver for your CD-ROM drive'. But what are the chances of that happening?

One approach is to establish who made the drive by looking in Device Manager, as described earlier. Make a note of the model. Now track down the company's website and look for a driver download area. Be sure to look for a DOS driver, not a Windows driver (which is quite different and useless in the present circumstances). Alternatively, try the following websites:

http://www.drivershq.com
http://www.driverzone.com

Once you have located and/or downloaded the appropriate driver, make a startup disk as described above. The procedure may vary slightly depending upon which version of Windows 95 you have. When that's done, copy the DOS driver onto the floppy disk.

Unfortunately, at this point you also have to manually edit some critical system files on the disk, and this is when it all gets horribly complicated. For the clearest walkthrough of the process around, visit Bob O'Donnell's page here:

http://www.everythingcomputers.com/windows_boot_disk.htm

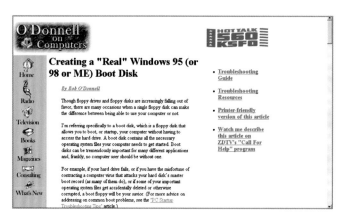

This site is also worth a visit, and it includes a file download to get your startup disk working with generic CD drives:

http://www.fixwindows.com/win95/cdboot.htm

Better still, upgrade to Windows 98, Millennium Edition or XP now and be done with this startup silliness!

TECHIE CORNER

Driver A driver is a software program that enables your PC's operating system to communicate with hardware devices. Most upgrades involve installing drivers. Without one in place, the computer either won't realise that it's just grown a new limb or will recognise that *something* has been bolted on but can't do a thing with it. New drivers are often written throughout the lifespan of a device and it pays to check the manufacturer's website from time to time. An updated driver will often fix problems with an earlier version or even add new functionality. However, updated drivers can also introduce new troubles, so only go down this route if you're having problems.

Backing up your files

Quite how you make copies of your valuable files depends largely upon your system. That is, if you have nothing but a floppy drive onboard, you're pretty well limited to shifting data in batches of 1.44MB of less (which equates to around 700 disks per gigabyte!). Zip drives, by contrast, use disks with capacities of 100 or 250MB, depending on the model, and a recordable CD drive lets you backup 650 or 700MB of data at a time (and quickly too). A tape drive offers even greater flexibility. Indeed, one of the best reasons for upgrading a PC is to improve your options for backing up data.

Do bear in mind the difference between backups and archives. Backing up your current company accounts onto a Zip disk and keeping it in a fire-proof safe protects you if your office burns down. Archiving data, on the other hand, is making a copy of information you want to hang on to but rarely need to use. Burning last year's accounts onto a CD-R means you can put the disk on the shelf and delete the file from your PC, freeing up space.

Getting your backup

One method is simply copying your files onto a floppy or Zip disk using Windows Explorer or My Computer. However, before you can copy files onto a recordable CD disc, you need to install what is known as a packet-writing program. This software is often included with new CD-R/RW drives. Windows XP very sensibly has packet-writing technology built in from the outset.

Alternatively, there are plenty of utility software programs around that automate the backup process. Some will even save your files to a floppy or Zip disk on the fly as you work.

Recordable compact discs are a cheap and efficient way to archive your old data.

TECHIE CORNER

Good housekeeping If you've ever performed a backup before, you'll appreciate the importance of good file management. There's nothing worse than spending an age and a half tracking down elusive documents with meaningless names secreted in obscure folders. Save yourself a headache by storing all of your files within one top-level folder. It doesn't matter how complex a hierarchy of sub and sub-sub folders you create so long as you can back up everything in one hit. *Never* store important data in the Windows folder (C:\Windows). If Windows breaks and has to be reinstalled, say sayonara to your work. Better by far to keep everything in the My Documents folder. That's what it's there for.

Windows 98 comes with its own utility called, unsurprisingly, Microsoft Backup. If it's already installed on your PC, you'll find it by clicking Start, Programs, Accessories and System Tools. If it's not there, open the Add/Remove Programs dialogue box (see p.25), click on the Windows Setup tab, and install Backup in the System Tools section. You'll need your original Windows CD-ROM disc. Unfortunately, Backup cannot be installed so easily under Windows Millennium Edition. What you have to do is dig out your original Windows Me installation CD-ROM, find the Add-ons/Msbackup folder, and double-click a file called Msbexp.exe. The beauty of Backup is that it supports disk spanning, which means that a backup job can be saved seamlessly across as many floppy or Zip disks as necessary. In other words, you can select as many files for backing up as you want to without worrying about their sizes: the program automatically asks for the requisite number of disks and saves the data piecemeal fashion.

Restoring data is essentially just a case of running Backup in reverse and inserting the floppy disks *in the right order* when prompted (which adds up to one very good reason for labelling them properly as you make the original backup!)

However, some important caveats: the Windows 95 version of Backup does *not* support removable drives like Zip or tape. See this web page for details:
http://support.microsoft.com/default.aspx?scit=kb;EN-GB;q135280
The Windows 98 version might not initially offer to use your Zip or tape drive, but it can be persuaded to do so. See:
http://support.microsoft.com/default.aspx?scit=kb;EN-GB;q186168
and:
http://support.microsoft.com/default.aspx?scit=kb;EN-GB;q188575

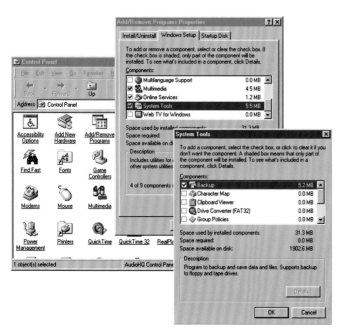

Backup is an optional extra in Windows but easily installed from the CD-ROM.

Good file management pays dividends when it comes to backing up your data.

PART  The tools you'll need

As we remarked earlier, fiddling with computers isn't rocket science. Nor is it brain surgery. It's a whole lot easier than replacing a car's suspension, or even the brakes on a bicycle, and it requires neither skill nor experience. Short of spilling your coffee over the motherboard, you're very unlikely to actually break your computer. However, do give yourself plenty of space to work. For even the simplest internal task, it's worthwhile shifting the whole shebang from a cramped desktop to somewhere more suitable. At the very least, ensure that you have sufficient room to work comfortably with a tower PC lying on its side.

If you can change a fuse, you can upgrade a computer.

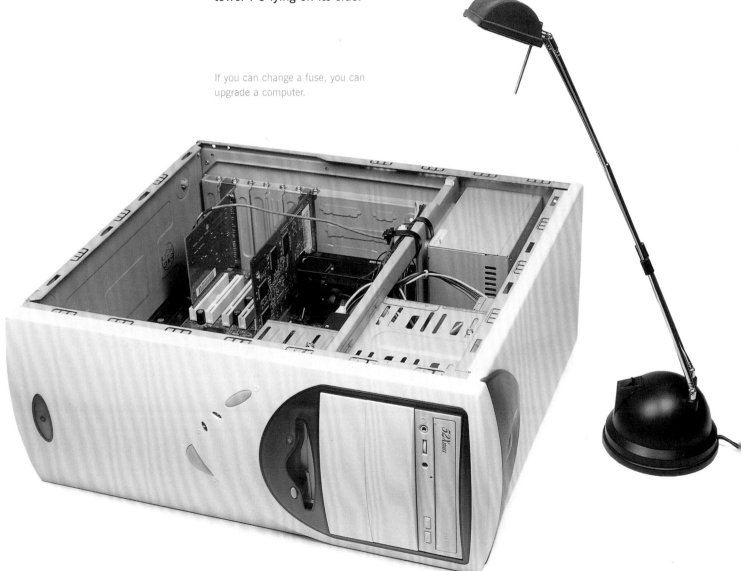

You'll need five tools to work on your PC's delicate innermost parts

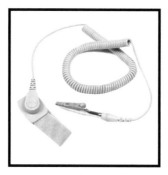

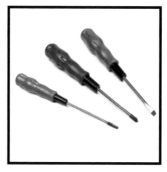

A manual *for your motherboard and, ideally, all the other manuals and paperwork that came with your PC and peripherals. If your motherboard is a mystery, download a copy of Sandra (see p.23) and run the Mainboard module. Now visit the manufacturer's website and cross your fingers that there's a downloadable manual available.*

An antistatic wrist-strap. *It won't save your life if you upgrade a running PC from the comfort of your bath but it will disperse any build-up of static electricity in your body and thus safeguard delicate circuitry from an unwelcome fry-up. Your computer will thank you for it – and so will your wallet. Wear one with pride.*

Screwdrivers. *One small Phillips will probably suffice – that's the one with the cross-shaped pointy end – but have a flathead screwdriver to hand just in case. If you can't resist, buy one of those handy 'PC upgrade' kits.*

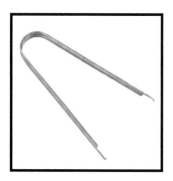

There's only one other must-have, and that's patience. Always a virtue, a measure of patience is truly essential when it comes to upgrading a PC. The task at hand might not be successful at the first attempt. You might have trouble installing drivers or any one of a million minor niggles may strike without warning. But don't rush it. Ever. Take your time, work through the manual that comes with any new device or component (even if it's written in Jargonese, as is the norm), and think logically. Don't replace your hard disk on a Monday morning or network the office on a Friday afternoon when you'd rather be elsewhere. There. Now are you ready to peek inside?

Tweezers *or delicate long-nosed pliers. Essential for retrieving dropped screws.*

A torch. *Miniaturisation ensures a surfeit of nooks and crannies inside your computer, and they're all dark.*

PART 1 Lifting the lid

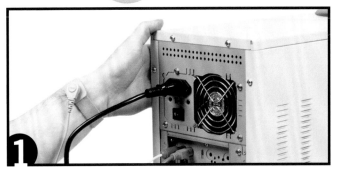  

Opinions vary on whether it's safer to leave the PC's case connected to the mains while you work – with the power turned off at the wall, of course – or to unplug it completely. Leaving it connected provides a path to earth for static electricity and protects the computer's components, so that's the approach that we'll adopt here. However, do feel free to unplug the machine completely if it makes you more comfortable – and certainly do this if there's no on/off switch at your wall socket.

Unplug all other cables and connectors from the back of the machine. If it helps, make a note of where everything goes, perhaps using sticky labels. In practice, thanks to myriad different interfaces present on the back of your PC, the plug on the end of a peripheral's cable will typically fit only one socket. See p158 for a guide.

Dig out the manual that came with your computer and figure out what holds it together. Yes, we know that sounds rather vague but there are any number of ways to screw a case together, and few of them are obvious. We've even seen designs where to get at the retaining screws you have to forcibly prise off the front of the case. Talk about counter-intuitive!

Touch something metal like a radiator to discharge any static electricity in your body. Before going near anything internally, put on your wrist-strap and connect it to a metal part of the case. Now peer inside. Does it look like the picture on the right? Good. Then it's definitely a computer. Now let's make it a better one.

PART **2**

Straight to the heart

You'd think, would you not, that the quickest way to speed up an ailing PC would be to give it a brainpower boost? Surprisingly, this isn't always – indeed, not even usually – the case: less radical measures are generally more effective and *much* easier.

PART  Motherboard architecture

If you understand the importance and role of the motherboard, you can do just about anything with a PC. Every area of this manual touches upon the motherboard in one way or another because this is the central component in a PC to which everything else is attached. In fact, installing a new motherboard is tantamount to building a PC from scratch rather than effecting an upgrade, and we look at this in some detail in Appendix 5 on p159.

Mouse and *keyboard* sockets.

USB two USB interfaces for connecting external devices.

Parallel port one parallel interface, usually reserved for the printer.

Serial port two serial interfaces for connecting external devices (hidden below parallel port).

Three good reasons to replace your motherboard

You want a faster computer It's possible to buy a motherboard with a processor already installed, which means that you don't have to fuss with BIOS upgrades, voltage concerns, system bus speeds and all the rest of that malarkey.

Your old motherboard has given up the ghost It's not a common failure, but it happens. If your PC is playing up, and you're sure it's down to the motherboard – remember, this can cause a number of problems, not all of them fatal – then the PC equivalent of open-heart surgery can save the day. Why not take the chance to upgrade to a better model at the same time?

You'd like to upgrade once and once only Some modern motherboards fully incorporate all the circuitry required for graphics and sound output, and sometimes even include a modem. This makes for an economical, relatively fuss-free route to a full multimedia system.

Three good reasons *not* to replace your motherboard

You may have to reformat your hard disk or at least reinstall Windows. The shock of finding a whole new motherboard under the hood can be too much for an operating system to bear.

Your old components may no longer fit. Will that old ISA soundcard find a home on your swanky new motherboard? What will you do with your PCI graphics card if the new motherboard has an AGP slot (see p.72)? And what about RAM? Chances are you'll have to chuck out all your old memory and buy it afresh to comply with the new standards. If you discover that you have to buy new components throughout, would it not be as cheap (and much easier) to start all over again with a new PC, perhaps hanging onto your old monitor, printer, keyboard and mouse to save a little cash? Hint: yes.

The motherboard itself may not fit. Computer cases are designed to accommodate motherboards of varying dimensions so it's never safe to assume that any old motherboard will feel at home in your PC. And what happens if the layout on the new motherboard is different and the case's power supply completely blocks access to the processor slot? You won't get very far with a brain-dead PC.

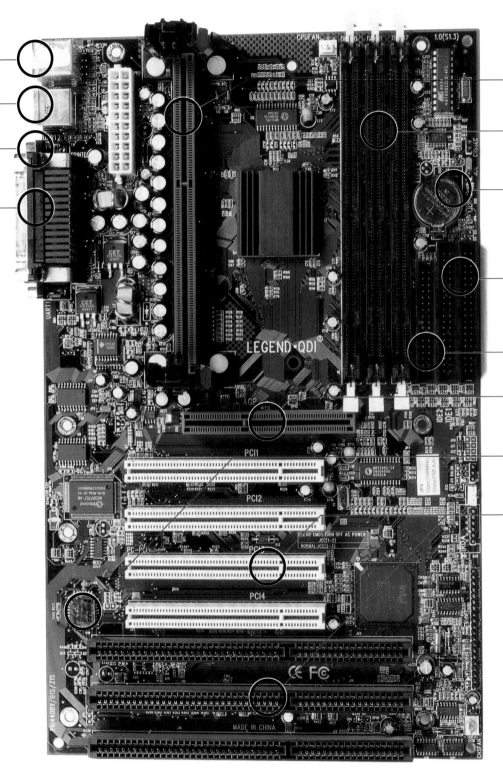

Slot 1 *this is the slot version of a processor connector*

Memory *this is where RAM is installed. In this case, we're looking at DIMM sockets.*

CMOS battery *a replaceable battery that keeps the CMOS alive when the power is switched off. Home to all your hardware settings (see p.153).*

IDE controllers *the hard disk plugs into one of these and the CD-ROM drive to the other. See p.46.*

Floppy disk controller *yes, the floppy disk drive plugs in here*

AGP slot *an expansion slot reserved for a high performance graphics card.*

BIOS *a memory chip that kick-starts a PC before Windows wakes up (see p.153).*

Expansion slots *a wide variety of expansion cards can be installed in these slots to add to a PC's features. We'll look at the different types in detail on p.72.*

PART ② Upgrading RAM

Your PC's operating system requires a good deal of RAM (Random Access Memory) to run smoothly. Windows 95 needs at least 8MB to work at all, 16MB to work properly, and double that again to work smoothly. Windows 98 demands at least 16MB to get out of bed, but 64MB is a realistic minimum. Windows Millennium Edition doesn't really perform with less than 128MB, and XP ups the ante again to a whopping 256MB. Bear in mind that this is before you do anything else, anything *useful*, with your PC like write a letter or send an email. Every program you fire up operates in RAM, and every document, picture or file resides there too for as long as it's 'open'.

DDR RAM.

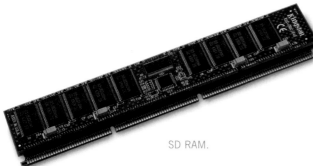

SD RAM.

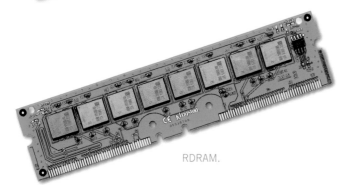

RDRAM.

When the available memory begins to run out, as it invariably does, the first thing you notice is a general slow down in operations. Come the point of RAM overload, the PC has four choices: give up and crash; freeze unhelpfully; refuse to do another thing until you close down some programs; or magic some more RAM out of thin air. Thankfully, the last option is first to be followed. Windows reserves an area of the hard disk for use as a kind of pretend, or virtual, memory (and calls it a swap file). This keeps things ticking over but it's woefully inefficient compared to using real RAM. If you hear your hard disk whirring and clicking a lot as you work, this is a sign of 'thrashing' – i.e. the disk struggling to keep up with the pressure as Windows constantly swaps data between it and RAM. Despite the name, it's not painful but it does nothing for performance.

All of which leads us to one inescapable conclusion: RAM is good, and more is better. What's more, it's also very straightforward to install extra memory.

What you need to know

Inevitably, RAM comes in assorted flavours and you have to be sure to buy the right type for your particular PC. Here's a guide to the critical specifications.

Capacity RAM is measured in megabytes and available in several sizes, including 4, 8, 16, 32, 64, 128, 256 and 512MB. We looked at how to establish how much RAM you already have onboard back on p.22.

Type Like everything else in the PC world, RAM has evolved apace. Brand new systems might come with souped up versions called RD or DDR RAM (Rambus Dynamic and Double Data Rate, as if you care), but your existing system will probably have SD (Synchronous Dynamic) RAM installed. It's time to check your motherboard manual, or dig out the order/delivery paperwork just to make sure.

Connector RAM comes in modules loaded with storage cells that slot into sockets on the motherboard. There are two main types: SIMM (Single Inline Memory Module) and DIMM (Dual Inline Memory Module). To fit a RAM upgrade, you either use a free

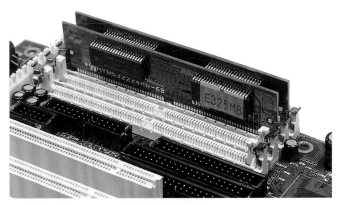

RAM modules sit in slots on the motherboard.

Windows uses the hard disk to make up for any RAM deficiency. A proper memory upgrade is much more efficient.

slot or, if necessary, replace an existing RAM module with a higher capacity version e.g. ditch a measly 16MB module to free up space for a 64MB module.

One complication, and an important one: SIMMs *must* be grouped together in pairs, or 'banks', where each module has the same capacity. The motherboard in a typical older Pentium PC would have four sockets (i.e. two banks), so possible configurations would include:

		or		
1st bank	2 x 16MB SIMMs	**1st bank**	2 x 16MB SIMMs
2nd bank	2 x 16MB SIMMs	**2nd bank**	2 x 32MB SIMMs
Total RAM	64MB	**Total RAM**	96MB

What you *can't* do is pluck one 16MB SIMM from its home and replace it with a 32MB module unless you simultaneously do the same with its partner. DIMMs have no such restriction. Curiously, Rambus memory complicates matters again. RIMM modules must be installed in matching pairs just like the old SIMMs, and you have to fill any unused sockets with dummy modules called Continuity RIMMs.

Speed It may seem odd to think of memory in terms of speed, but RAM modules talk to the processor at different rates. This is important because it relates to the speed of the chipset on the motherboard, so again check the manual and be sure to buy the fastest RAM that the motherboard supports.

PART ② Step-by-step RAM upgrade

1

2

3

Here we install a new 64Mb SD RAM module in a free DIMM socket.

Before attempting any internal work on your PC, re-read the safety precautions on p.31.

Ensure that you have clear access to the RAM sockets. This might mean temporarily removing other components.

The DIMM socket has a locking tab at either end. Press these down to the open position – i.e. angled away from the socket.

 TECHIE CORNER

SIMMs, DIMMs and RIMMs too
How do you tell a DIMM from a SIMM? Simple: both have notches roughly in the centre on their connecting edges but only a DIMM has an extra off-centre notch to ensure that you can't plug it into the motherboard the wrong way around. Note that DIMMS always install vertically (i.e. perpendicular to the motherboard) but SIMMs usually install at an angle. Instead of locking tabs, SIMM sockets generally have retaining clips at either end. Finally, DIMMs are bigger, and have 168 rather than 72 connecting pins along their base.

So what's a RIMM? Simpler still: it's a proprietary superfast design developed by a company called Rambus, licensed to other manufacturers and only found on the very latest Pentium 4 systems.

SIMM.

DIMM.

RIMM.

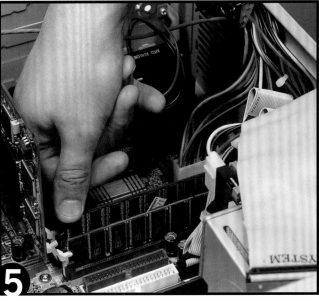

4

5

Line up *the notches on the connecting edge of the DIMM with the socket and insert it, keeping the module vertical. Note the off-centre notch that dictates which way around the module fits. If necessary, use a gentle end-to-end rocking motion to seat it in the socket.*

Push *the locking tabs home to secure the DIMM. If they won't lock, press down* gently *on the DIMM to push it fully home.*

When you restart the computer, watch the screen carefully. When the system runs through its standard memory test, just check that the total RAM reported is now 64MB greater than it was. Many PCs will say System Configuration Updated (or some such message) and may require you to press a key in acknowledgement. And that's it: no fuss with drivers, no fiddly configuration, just a much improved PC. Enjoy.

All you'll ever want to know about memory can be found here:
http://www.kingston.com/tools/umg/default.asp
Specific memory questions are answered here:
http://support.crucial.com

TROUBLE-SHOOTER

If the RAM upgrade does not register when you start the system, check the details in the General tab of Device Manager (see P.22). If this looks right, reboot and try again.
Still not registering? Repeat the installation process and ensure that the new module is properly locked in place.
If this is a SIMM upgrade, check that you've followed the bank rules, i.e. installed two SIMMs of equal capacity in each bank.
As a final test, remove the new module and move one of the existing modules (DIMM only) into the now-vacant socket. Restart and ensure that the original

quantity RAM still registers. This way, you'll confirm that a) you're doing everything correctly; b) the socket itself is fine; c) the new module must be faulty. Exchange it!

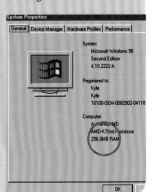

PART

Understanding processors

Imagine this manual was double its current size. Now double it again. Now cram it full of hieroglyphic tables, small print, warnings, disclaimers and impenetrable jargon. You *still* wouldn't have enough information on hand to perform a processor upgrade in all possible circumstances. There are just too many angles, too many possibilities, too many permutations to cover all bases. This book is much too short to make such an attempt. So is life. But surely, you protest, it's merely a matter of out with the old and in with the new? How hard can it be? Well, the physical procedure for changing the component is indeed straightforward, as we shall see, but *getting* to that point is fraught with difficulties. The first really seriously limiting factor is whether a new processor will even fit onto your existing motherboard.

Die used to make Pentium 4 chips.

The most common connectors

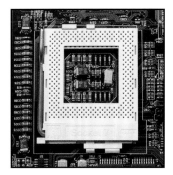

Socket 7 – *a flat socket on the motherboard. Compatible processors include: Pentium and Pentium MMX; AMD K6; Cyrix 6x86 MX and MII.*

Slot 1 – *a groove in which the processor cartridge sits on edge. Compatible processors include: Intel Celeron, Pentium II and Pentium III.*

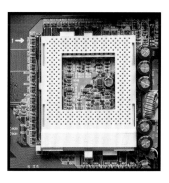

Socket 370 – *a newer style socket. Compatible processors include: Intel Celeron and Pentium III (yes, these two ranges are available in both slot and socket designs).*

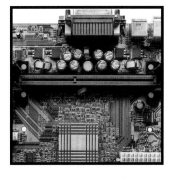

Slot A – *similar to Slot 1 but designed exclusively for AMD's Athlon and Duron ranges.*

Socket A *(also known as Socket 462) – an alternative socket approach for AMD Athlon and Duron processors. There are in fact several other designs but the point holds true throughout: only a processor designed for a particular socket or slot can be used in an upgrade.*

TECHIE CORNER

The good news is that most post-Pentium processors are perfectly fast enough to cope with most computer work, short of running intensive multimedia applications and playing the latest games. If it's graphical performance you need, consider installing a new graphics card instead (p.74). The benefits will be far greater than those to be had by swapping the processor alone. Likewise, a PC's overall performance can be better improved by increasing the amount of RAM on tap (p.36), because this gives it more working space.

Remember all that 'Apollo missions were run on a calculator' stuff from the opening pages? It's time for a reality check. Do you really need a processor running at two billion clock cycles per second? No, you don't. Or if your computer usage is so intensive and demanding that you really *do* need a super-super-superfast processor at the helm, then you also need a brand new state-of-the-art system crammed with the latest complementary devices to support it. In other words, forget about an upgrade and buy a new system instead.

More things to worry about

The slot/socket compatibility issue is only one consideration. Others include:

System bus speed (also known as the front side bus). The rate at which data is handled by the motherboard, which determines the true speed of a PC. A processor can work flat out for all its worth but if the motherboard (or, more precisely, the chipset) can't process its results quickly enough, that equates to a lot of wasted effort. Most motherboards include a feature called a multiplier that enables them to accept faster processors than they were originally designed for, but there are constraints – see Techie Corner on p.43.

Cooling Faster processors require more cooling, either in the form of a heatsink (a solid-state contraption that dissipates heat through convection), or a fan, or both. Do without and it'll all go up in smoke. Literally.

The BIOS chip (see p.153) on the motherboard may not recognise the new processor, in which case it also needs an upgrade. If you want the PC to restart, and we imagine that you do, this must be done before you start work on the processor.

Voltages Does your motherboard support the required voltage of the processor? As a rule, modern processors run at lower voltages (i.e. cooler) than their predecessors, and a 3.3v model will soon blow up or burn out in a 5v socket. It's vital to check that your motherboard and processor upgrade are compatible.

A motherboard bus.

BIOS (Basic Input/Output System) is a chip on the motherboard that controls the fundamental operations of a computer.

DO consider replacing the entire motherboard replete with a new processor. It's more expensive but takes care of most worries in a single move. Is there any point jazzing up just one component if everything else remains in place? A fast processor in an old system will run like a Ferrari in a car park. See Appendix 5 on p159 for more information on installing a new motherboard.

Speed demon For all their power, processors deal exclusively in the 1s and 0s of binary code. That in itself sounds baffling until you consider that a 1 is merely a signal generated by an electric current, and a 0 the lack of such a signal. The code 101, for instance, translates as power on-off-on again. The processor then runs these signals through its many, many microscopic transistors, interprets them according to certain logical rules, and outputs a binary response. Simple, huh? It's all controlled by an internal clock (of sorts) that beats at a certain rate. A 500MHz processor ticks 500 million (yes, *million*) times every single second, with each tick representing an opportunity for the processor to do something useful. Thus a 500MHz processor can do more work in a shorter time than a 200MHz model.

It's not *all* about speed, but even a cursory glance at processor technology takes you deep into a world that you really don't want to visit. Instead, here's a ready reckoner of how quickly Intel Pentium processors have evolved.

Pentium
1993
60–200MHz

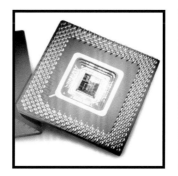

Pentium Pro
1995
150–200MHz

Pentium MMX
1997
166–233MHz

Pentium II
1997
233–450MHz

TECHIE CORNER

ZIF stands for Zero Insertion Force. Rather than having to forcibly pry a processor out of its socket with clumsy, nervy fingers, a lever unlocks it so you can simply lift the chip out. Older PCs often have a LIF (the L's for Low) socket instead, in which case there's no lever and you need a special tool called a (wait for it) chip remover to gently prise the processor free. Be careful when putting a processer into a Low Insertion Force socket – the force required is not at all that low and is perilously close to that required to crack the motherboard. Intel

recommends against home relpacements of LIF chips – good advice that we endorse.

System Bus We mentioned the importance of system bus above. Now here's how it works. A motherboard will work with a processor that runs at a speed equivalent to the system bus speed multiplied by a factor of 0.5 and increments thereof. That is, a 60MHz bus is compatible with a 90MHz processor (60 x 1.5 = 90) or a 150MHz processor (60 x 2.5 = 150). It is not, however, compatible with a 200MHz processor, simply because 200 is not a multiple of 60.
The earliest Pentiums ran with a system bus of 60MHz, soon superceded by 66M, 100 and 133MHz. As we write, the latest generation of Pentium 4 processors use a system bus speed of 533MHz.

Pentium III
1999
450–1.13GHz

Pentium 4
2000
1.3–2.53 GHz . . . and rising

43

PART **3** COMPUTER MANUAL

Adding a new drive

Breathing new life into an ailing PC with major surgery is one thing, but there's more than one way to skin a cat (or mix a metaphor). Some of these upgrades will boost its performance, others will prolong its useful lifespan, but all will make your PC a more productive tool and/or a better toy.

PART 3

A word about channels

When it comes to installing a new hard disk or, indeed, any other kind of internal drive like a CD-ROM or DVD drive, the first consideration is how to connect it to the rest of the computer system. What it needs is an interface of some description, and this is where the notion of channels comes in.

A channel is a gateway that enables the exchange of data between the drive and the rest of the PC through the motherboard. The connection point itself – basically a smart plug socket – is called a host adaptor. There are (of course) two possibilities.

IDE (Integrated Drive Electronics)

The most common interface for hard disk and CD drives, IDE hides under various nicknames (see Techie Corner on opposite page). Virtually all motherboards have one or two IDE adaptors onboard, depending upon their age. We'll assume that you have two. In most cases, the hard disk will be connected to one controller and the CD-ROM drive to the other, both by means of flat, wide ribbon-like cables. If you examine each ribbon, you may or may not find a spare connector somewhere along its length. This is because each IDE channel can host two separate

IDE adaptors should be clearly marked on the motherboard. If not, they're easy enough to find.

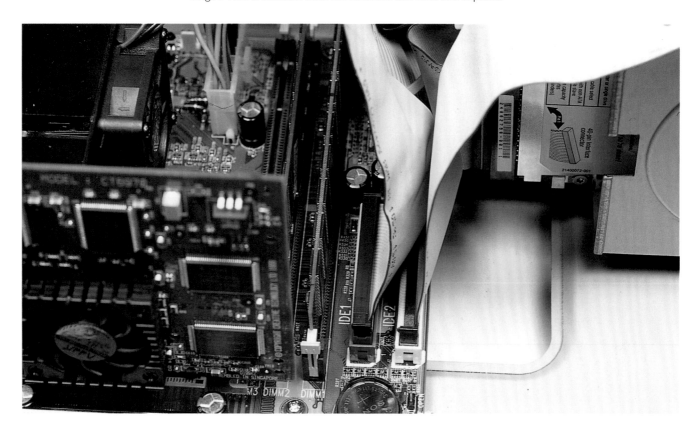

The 'pin 1' edge of an IDE cable is colour-coded. You must match this with pin 1 on your drive and the motherboard.

drives, one of which is designated the *master* and the other the *slave*. This allows a total of four drives to be connected to the motherboard. The master/slave nomenclature is actually rather misleading, as it merely indicates the order in which Windows allocates drive letters to devices (C: to the master drive, then D: to the slave or, if there is no slave, the next master drive).

If a ribbon in your PC does *not* have a spare connector, you'll need to replace it before installing an extra drive. Often, but not always, a spare ribbon is included in the box with a new drive; otherwise, get yourself a 40-wire/80-pin ribbon equipped with three connectors.

Note one very important point: the IDE ribbon cable is coloured pink or red along one edge. This corresponds to 'pin 1' and is there to ensure that you connect the cable correctly. Always carefully identify the pin 1 position on both your device and the motherboard before plugging in a cable. It should be clearly marked but you may have to consult the manual.

The advantages of going down the IDE route are pretty compelling: your PC already has the requisite adaptors in place, and the vast majority of drives come ready equipped to plug in and play with a minimum of fuss. However...

SCSI (Small Computer System Interface, but just call it 'scuzzy')

SCSI is an alternative channel with one big benefit over IDE, namely that multiple devices can share a single adaptor. So, instead of a maximum of four devices sharing two IDE channels, a SCSI-equipped PC can have 7 or 15 devices all daisy-chained together – or even more if it has a second SCSI adaptor. What's more, SCSI drives can be considerably faster than their IDE counterparts.

But there are disadvantages. One is simply the cost: gigabyte for gigabyte, SCSI devices are more expensive to buy. The other is that motherboards do not generally come with a SCSI adaptor onboard, which means that you have to fit one yourself before installing a SCSI device. This is as simple as fitting an expansion card, of which much more shortly, but it does use up a free expansion slot and adds considerably to the cost (and hassle).

Besides which, the difference in speed between a SCSI and an IDE drive is negligible in normal use, and it's really only servers that benefit from multiple device support. We'll assume here that IDE is your chosen course.

A SCSI adaptor expansion card adds a new dimension to your drive possibilities but it's far from essential in a domestic computer.

TECHIE CORNER

IDE standards Just one IDE standard? That'll be the day! Here's a summary of the main specifications in the order in which they appeared. Forget what they mean, how they evolved and why they matter: when buying a new drive, just make sure you choose one that matches your motherboard's particular flavour of IDE support (time to check that manual again). Or check the stickers on your existing drives and buy like for like.

IDE	ATA-1
EIDE	Fast ATA-2
EIDE Ultra33	ATA/33
EIDE Ultra66	ATA/66
EIDE Ultra100	ATA/100
EIDE Ultra133	ATA/133
ATAPI	an IDE standard that supports devices other than hard disks like CD-ROM and DVD drives.

Oh, and ATA is sometimes called DMA (or UDMA) instead.

Why upgrade your hard disk?

Here's a funny thing: no matter why you first bought your PC, you're almost certainly using it for something entirely different now. As we become more proficient and confident, we explore new avenues and discover just what all this hardware and software can really do for us. Thus it's no surprise to find a book-keeping machine roped into editing digital video or a system purchased primarily for internet access functioning as a full-blown home entertainment centre. That's why upgrading a PC is so often a compelling, and frequently pressing, affair.

One of the key components that comes under pressure soonest is the hard disk. It's amazing just how quickly a seemingly cavernous disk can fill to capacity. A single megabyte might be sufficient storage space for the entire text of a novel, but that equates to a mere six seconds or so of uncompressed music. Throw in a few high resolution images or video files and take into account the size of modern software applications, including the operating system itself, and it's little wonder that we run out of space sooner than we thought possible. This is when our thoughts turn to upgrading the hard disk.

When your hard disk falls behind the times, it's time to upgrade.

External hard disks are portable, practical – and pricey.

Zip drives are ideal for backing up 100 or 250MB of data at a time.

For mass storage, nothing beats a tape drive.

How to upgrade…

There are essentially three upgrade options. First, you might install a secondary hard disk alongside your existing one, akin to building a warehouse in the car park. Alternatively, you might prefer to *replace* your existing hard disk. This has the virtue of neatness but the distinct disadvantages that you must also reinstall the operating system from scratch and somehow transfer all your existing files onto the new disk. We'll cover this in detail on p54. Of course, if your original disk was to suddenly fail – a rare occurrence but always a possibility – this might be your only option.

Finally, you might plump for an external hard disk. Such a solution costs more to buy, and gets even more expensive if you have to buy a special controller card on top. If it connects to the PC through a slower external parallel or USB interface, it will be much slower at saving data too. Then again, a FireWire or external SCSI drive can offer higher speeds than a plain old IDE drive. What's more, you can take the entire shebang with you wherever you wander and quickly plug it into any other PC. What better way to carry 20GB of data in your pocket?

…and how not to

If storage space is your only concern, do consider some form of removable media. For instance, a recordable CD drive could be used to permanently archive all your older files and thus lighten the load on the hard disk. A high-end Zip drive is another possibility (250MB per disk), as are Jaz (2GB per cartridge) and tape drives (60GB with ease).

Windows also provides a few good simple tools that can make a big difference to a hard disk's performance *and* free up considerable space. Don't spend a penny before reading Part 7.

Iomega's Jaz drive holds a massive 2GB per cartridge.

What you need to know

The hard disk is a device used for storing data. Unlike RAM,
where data is held in a kind of dynamic flux, files once saved to
the hard disk are housed in safe storage. These files can, of
course, be retrieved from the hard disk and altered, deleted or
simply re-saved at will, but they don't disappear when the power
is switched off. The hard disk *drive* is the mechanism that
controls the disk, including the magnetic heads that do the hard
work and the case in which it's all held. But since the disk and
the drive are in practice inseparable, we'll just talk about disks.

As well as choosing between an IDE or SCSI interface and
getting to grips with the EIDE/ATA/DMA muddle, certain other
specifications should be considered before you go shopping.

Capacity Without question, size matters when it comes to hard
disks. Modern disks can top 80GB and we'd certainly suggest
that 20GB is the absolute minimum for a secondary disk.

Speed #1 Not an obvious consideration, perhaps, but hard disks
spin at different rates. You'll see rotational (or spindle) speeds of
5,400, 7,200 and 10,000rpm, and it doesn't hurt to get the
nimblest disk that you can afford because the faster the disk spins,
the faster it can spit out data to your eagerly waiting computer.
Note, however, that it's never worth upgrading a hard disk for
speed alone. We're talking about differences on the scale of
milliseconds.

Mounting brackets enable a 3.5 inch drive to use a 5.25 inch bay.

Speed #2 The speed that matters more involves something called direct memory access (DMA), a process whereby data moves from the hard disk into RAM without going through the processor. Look for ratings of 33, 66, 100 and even 133 megabytes per second. But even if the faster option is within budget, check the rating of the hard disk controller on your motherboard. Installing a fast disk on a slow motherboard is a waste of time.

Drive size Internal hard disks are 3.5 inch drives. This is fine so long as you have a free 3.5 inch drive bay available – and you'll probably have to open up the case to find out – but otherwise you'll need a special mounting bracket to secure it in a 5.25 inch bay. Such a bracket may or may not come in the box, so check first.

Setup software New hard disks must be formatted before they work, and some come with their own setup software that makes this a breeze. Check – and go for the easy option every time!

A word of warning

If your motherboard is of a certain age, there may be three distinct problems with its BIOS. On one hand, it may not recognise disks larger than 504MB, in which case your new toy is going to be invisible to the PC. On another hand, if the BIOS is a little younger but still no spring chicken, it may not recognise disks larger than 8GB – in which case ditto. However, many drives come with slick software that can circumvent these issues, or you could always upgrade the BIOS first. Note that if your motherboard has EIDE controllers onboard (as opposed to plain IDE), no problem: your BIOS is just fine.

But on the third and final hand, only a 'plug and play' BIOS chip will automatically recognise a new hard disk and supply CMOS (see Appendix 2 on p.153) with all the information it needs (specifically, how many cylinders, heads and sectors the disk has). Failing that, you'll have to manually enter all this stuff in CMOS yourself. Although this isn't actually too difficult, it can seem a daunting, non-intuitive procedure for a novice and we wouldn't recommend it unless you're absolutely confident of getting it right. Our advice would be to consider an internal hard disk upgrade only if you are sure your BIOS supports large drives and recognises them automatically.

Check the specification carefully before buying a new hard disk.

PART ③ Step-by-step hard disk upgrade

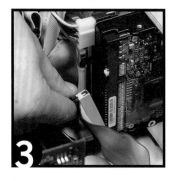

Before attempting any internal work on your PC, re-read the safety precautions on p.31.

Make sure that you can access the drive bay. Sometimes this means removing a plastic cover on the front of the case. Also check how to secure the disk in place. Usually this is a simple case of inserting screws on either side of the bay, but occasionally a sliding rail mechanism is used instead. Position the disk in its bay.

A secondary hard disk should be installed on the same IDE channel as the primary disk, which means that it should use the same ribbon cable. So, follow the ribbon cable from the existing disk all the way back to the motherboard and check that there's a spare connector.

While you're here, double-check that there's a spare power lead within reach. This is a 4-wire cable with a white connector (identical to those already supplying power to the primary disk and CD-ROM drive). If there's no spare lead, purchase a Y-shaped 'splitter' that turns one connector into two.

A splitter overcomes a shortage of power cables.

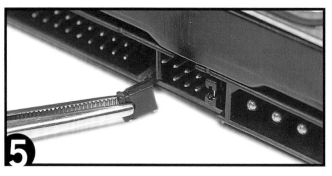

Having ascertained that you can fit and secure the disk, remove it and look around the back. Here you will find a number of metal pins and a plastic 'shunt' or two. These are jumpers, used to determine whether this is going to be the master or the slave device on this IDE channel. The primary hard disk – i.e. the disk that contains Windows – is always the master. Therefore, as we are installing a secondary hard disk for storage purposes only, it's the slave. Check the settings on both disks on the channel – sometimes you have to adjust your existing drive, too, if it has been configured to be the only drive on the channel. Check the manual that came with the disk for instructions on how to set the jumpers appropriately. You may also find a jumper guide printed on the hard disk casing.

Now reinsert the drive, attach the ribbon cable and power leads gently but firmly, and secure the disk in place. If you're screwing it in place, make sure you don't over-tighten the screws as they mustn't poke too deeply into the bowels of the drive. Take a deep breath, put it all back together again, and restart the computer.

TECHIE CORNER

Fat disks and FAT Quite aside from any BIOS limitations, the very first release of Windows 95 did not support the use of the FAT 32 (file allocation table) file system. But the second release – Windows 95 OSR2, or just Windows 95b – did, as do Windows 98 Millennium Edition and XP. The important point is that only FAT32 systems can recognise hard disks larger than 2.1GB, which limits the attraction of an upgrade if you're still stuck with the original Windows 95.

What happens next?

This depends upon whether you have a plug and play BIOS chip on your motherboard. If so, lucky you: the computer now detects the presence of the new disk. If *not*, you'll have to manually enter details about the disk in CMOS (see Appendix 2), and you're most certainly going to need the documentation that came with the hard disk.

This may seem like an awful palaver. That's because it is an awful palaver. Here comes another one…

Partitioning and formatting your new hard disk

We'll look at the merits of sub-dividing a hard disk into manageable chunks later (see Appendix 3 on p155) but for now simply note that you have to first partition and then format your new component before you can do anything with it. This is when its own specialist setup software or a third party utility can make life much easier. However, we'll assume here that you have neither.

Click Start, point to Run, and then type command. At a command prompt, type **fdisk**, and then press **ENTER**. As the program starts, it will ask you if you want to enable large disk support. With a new drive, you will always want to do this, so type **Y**. The fdisk program will continue loading and then display the above menu.

Press 5, and then press **ENTER**. When you do this, the selection changes from the physical disk 1 (master) to the physical disk 2 (slave).

Press 2 and press **ENTER**.

Press 1 to select the Create DOS partition or Logical DOS Drive menu option.

Press ENTER.

Press 2 to select the Create Extended DOS Partition menu option.

Press ENTER.

Restart your computer to start Windows.

NB: For more in-depth instructions on partitioning and formatting, Microsoft provides an excellent article in its Knowledge Base on the web. You can find it at:

http://support.microsoft.com/default.aspx?scid=kb;EN-US;q255867

Migrating from one disk to another

As we mentioned on p49, the problem with replacing your existing hard disk with a fresh model is that you have to reinstall everything from scratch. But why? You might reasonably expect that you could install the new disk in the computer and simply copy all your data across from one to the other

Well, indeed you can, but only up to a point. Copy or moving files and folders from disk to disk is as simple as dragging and dropping icons in My Computer or Windows Explorer, but applications are not so easily shifted. The trouble is that when you install an application, it tends to deposit bits and pieces of itself all over the place. This makes it well nigh impossible to copy the application wholesale later, leaving you little option but to reinstall it afresh on the new disk. That may not sound too arduous but it means that you must still have the original CD-ROM in your possession and often involves a good deal of fiddling with configuration settings and customisable options before you have it working the way you're used to. Multiply this process ten or twenty-fold and suddenly you're faced with hours or even days of boring tweaking.

Worse, the operating system requires key system files that can not be copied while in use, which makes it impossible to move Windows between disks while Windows itself is running. And, of course, when Windows is not running, you can't do anything at all with your computer! Just consider how much time you've already spent setting up Windows to your liking, adjusting regional settings, downloading patches and fixes from the internet and generally customising your PC. It's back to square one with a new disk.

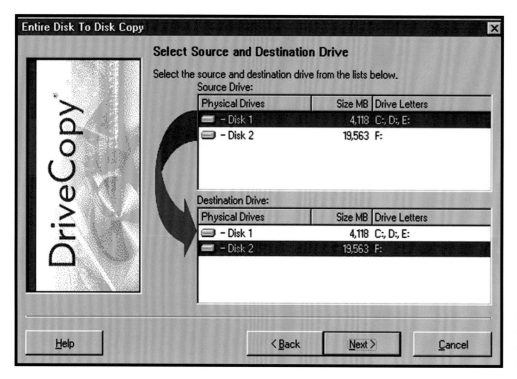

Specialist utility software makes it easy to migrate the contents of one hard disk to another, up to and including the operating system

Utility software

Or would be, were it not for the wonder of utility software. As a rule, when upgrading or maintaining computers, we like to keep expense to an absolute minimum, but there are occasions when a helping hand is truly welcome. This is one such occasion.

Hard disk 'cloning' tools like PowerQuest's Drive Image or Norton's Ghost let you backup an entire disk onto removable media like CD-R discs. These clone, or image, files can then be loaded onto the new disk and everything will – or should – look and work exactly as it did before.

An alternative and, in our view, safer and more effective approach is to use a dedicated disk migration tool like PowerQuest's DriveCopy. Here, you install the new disk on the same IDE channel as the original disk and set the jumpers appropriately to make it the slave device. When you reboot, DriveCopy kicks in before Windows starts and copies every shred of data from the original disk to the new one, including the operating system in its entirety. All you have to do now is swap the jumper settings around and the new disk immediately takes on the identity of C: drive. The original hard disk may either be kept as a backup device or removed from the computer.

However, do bear in mind that there may be times when it is actually preferable to start with a 'clean' operating system. Your existing copy of Windows might have a niggling fault that you simply can't resolve, or your computer might have contracted a deep-rooted virus that you'd rather be without.

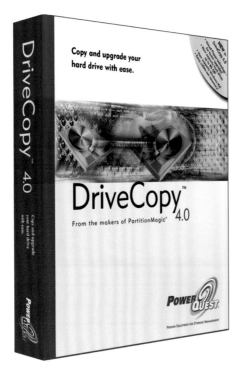

Disk cloning or copying tools make light work of installing a new hard disk

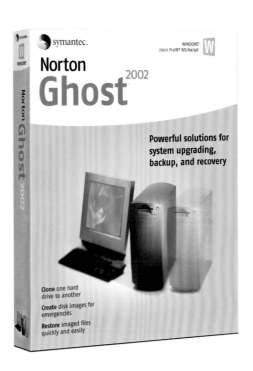

PART  Upgrading your CD-ROM drive

There are three reasons why you might consider upgrading your CD-ROM drive (apart from hardware failure, of course): to install software more quickly; to play CD-based games more smoothly; or to add extra features.

Like everything else, CD-ROM standards have evolved and today's drives are very much faster than yesterday's. Naturally enough, a fast drive can transfer data into the main computer system more quickly than a slow drive, so you'll see a big difference when you install a program on the scale of, say, an office suite. But just how often do you do that? And are you prepared to pay a good deal of money to save yourself five or ten minutes once or twice a year? We rather suspect not.

Most modern 3D action games are designed to run on quad speed (known as 4x) drives, or occasionally 8x. While a faster drive certainly can't hurt, a good games machine will benefit far more from a turbocharged graphics card and superfast processor than a mere CD-ROM upgrade.

No, the only really good reason to rip out a functioning CD-ROM drive is to add to your computer's powers. That's exactly what we'll look at here: adding a *recordable* CD drive.

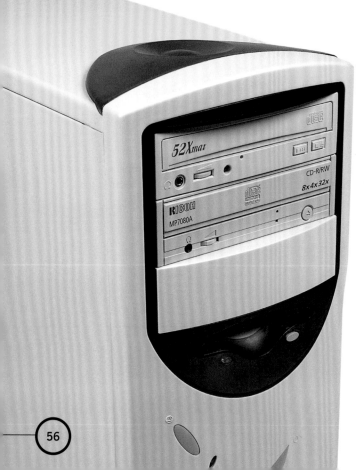

A recordable CD drive gives you better backup options – and makes audio and video CDs to boot.

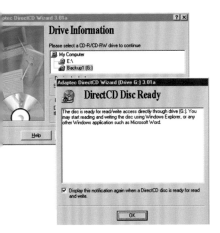

Packet writing software lets you fill a CD in bits and pieces rather than all at once.

Recordable drives

A CD-ROM drive can read data stored on standard CD-ROM discs such as those used to distribute software programs. It can also read audio CDs and relay the signal to a sound card in order for your PC to play music. What it expressly can *not* do is record data onto a disc. For that, you need either a CD-Recordable (CD-R) or a CD-Rewriteable (CD-RW) drive. The difference is simply this: CD-R drives use discs that can be recorded on to once and once only, whereas CD-RW drives use discs that can be re-recorded many times over. In fact, a CD-RW drive also works with CD-R discs, making it by far the better buy now that there is no appreciable price difference between the two technologies.

A single recordable disc holds at least 650MB of data – that's a massive 450 times more stuff than fits on a floppy disk – so the potential for archiving old files and making critical backups should be clear. Furthermore, with the right software it's easy to record your own audio compilations that can be played on household stereo equipment (note that some older car stereos won't play CD-R audio CDs) or copy existing CDs as long as you don't infringe copyright. You can even make video CDs that can be played in a domestic DVD player and watched on the television screen.

Drive	Media	Pros	Cons
CD-ROM (read-only memory)	Reads any standard CD-ROM or audio disc. Will also read 'finished' CD-R discs and *may* read CD-RW discs (no guarantee)	Essential equipment in any PC	Can not record (save) files onto disc
CD-R (recordable)	As above but also records on blank CD-R discs. These discs can be filled in a series of distinct sessions or piecemeal using packet writing software	Ideal for backing up and archiving data, copying discs and making audio and video compilations	Once full, a CD-R disc can not be re-recorded
CD-RW (rewriteable)	As above but records on both blank CD-R and reusable CD-RW discs	Maximum flexibility as you can use CD-R or CD-RW discs to suit the task in hand	Audio CD-RW discs are not always playable on domestic stereo equipment. Older CD-ROM drives can also struggle with CD-RW discs

CD-Rs can be written to multiple times until they are full. However, each extra 'session' you add to the disc has an overhead of 13MB so it's not ideal for adding lots of little files all the time. But thanks to the minor miracle of 'packet writing' software, now you can treat a CD-R or CD-RW disc just like a giant floppy and fill it up piece by piece, file by file. You might, for instance, make a daily backup of your critical work documents.

Add or replace? It's perfectly possible to install a CD-RW drive (or CD-R – the process is identical) alongside an existing CD-ROM drive but there's little or no point. For one thing, your new recordable drive also functions as a CD-ROM drive, and is likely to be a good deal faster than the old one. For another, replacing the drive means that you save both an IDE channel (more on this in a moment) and a drive bay (ditto). Also, to play audio discs, including multimedia presentations like encyclopaedias, the drive must connect to the sound card. Some cards only support one device which effectively renders one or other of the drives mute. Besides all of which, it's just as easy, if not easier, to make a direct swap – and isn't that what it's all about?

The one exception would be if you're planning to make regular copies of CDs. In this case, it's worth keeping the old drive for direct CD-to-CD copying, as otherwise the data has to be extracted from the original disc and written to the hard disk before a recording can commence.

TECHIE CORNER

Optical media Broadly speaking, two methods of data storage are used in a computer system: *magnetic* media, as in the hard and floppy disks; and *optical* media, as in a compact disc (recordable or otherwise). Optical in this context means that a laser reads light patterns reflected by the disc. In a recordable drive, the laser writes data to the disc by 'burning' pits in a malleable layer. This is quite a different process to that used in industry, where compact discs are pressed rather than burned, but the effect is much the same. Incidentally, as a rule (and a perfectly silly one at that) the term *disc* is generally used when referring to optical media like CDs and *disk* when referring to magnetic media. That's the convention we're following here. For more on CD technology, start here: **http://www.cdrfaq.org/ http://www.pctechguide.com/ 08cd-rom.htm http://www.pcguide.com/ref/cd**

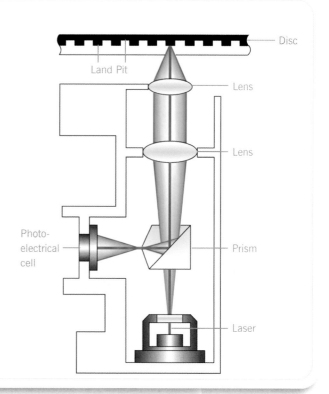

Disc

Land Pit

Lens

Lens

Photo-electrical cell

Prism

Laser

What you need to know

Praise be, recordable CD specs are nowhere near as complicated as you might expect. The critical considerations are these:

Speed A drive's speed is primarily a measure of how quickly the disc spins and therefore how quickly data is read and passed to the main system. It's a *little* more complicated than that – there's all that business about variable and constant velocities, seek times and access times – but let's not worry about it. The first generation of CD-ROM drives transferred data at a rate of 150 Kilobytes per second, referred to hereafter as 1x speed. Later models spin the discs faster – 2x, 4x, 8x, 12x, 16x, 24x, 32x and so on – with corresponding improvements in performance. However, 16x is generally regarded as quite fast enough for practical purposes so don't get hung up on drives claiming ludicrous and largely pointless 100x speeds.

Note that a CD-RW drive has three speed ratings: read, record (or write) and rewrite. These are usually expressed as, for example, 24x/8x/4x, which describes the drive's performance as a CD-ROM, CD-R and CD-RW device in that order. A CD-R drive has only read and record (write) speeds.

Media As discussed above, different drives work with different types of discs. CD-RW is the most flexible because it can read CD-ROM and audio discs and record on both recordable (cheap) and rewriteable (not so cheap) discs. However, CD-R discs offer greater compatibility and are thus better suited to audio compilations, transferring files from one PC to another and sharing data with others. Size-wise, blank discs generally have a capacity of 650MB (equivalent to 74 minutes of music) or 700MB (80 minutes) and are priced accordingly. CD-R discs are also speed rated. You must match the media to the writing speed that you will use, such as 12x.

Blank recordable discs are now affordable and reliable. Choose CD-R for maximum compatibility.

ADDING A NEW DRIVE

Step-by-step CD-RW drive upgrade

1

Before attempting any internal work on your PC, re-read the safety precautions on p.31.

2

The existing CD-ROM drive is wired up to a power supply, a ribbon cable connected to an IDE controller on the motherboard and an audio cable connected to the sound card. Unplug the cables from the drive (not the motherboard!) but keep the connectors within reach. You'll need them again in a moment.

3

The drive is secured in the bay with four short screws, two on either side. Remove these and set aside, and slide the drive forward until it's free.

...and more of what you need to know

Interface Like the hard disk, an internal CD drive connects to the rest of the computer through a channel (see p.46). This may either be IDE – in fact, a specific IDE standard know as ATAPI – or SCSI. There are benefits to be had from installing a SCSI drive but this invariably means installing a SCSI controller expansion card first (although some sound cards actually have a SCSI adaptor built in for just this purpose). We'll go down the more common IDE/ATAPI route here.

Drive bay CD drives of all persuasions use the standard 5.25 'half height' inch drive bay (see p.19). Assuming that your PC already has a CD-ROM drive installed, there will almost certainly be at least one free drive bay either above or below it. You may have to prise or snap off a plastic cover to gain access. In this example, of course, we're going to use the old drive's bay for the new device.

Alternatively, you could buy an *external* recordable CD drive for added convenience and portability. Parallel drives are painfully slow, USB less so, and FireWire almost as speedy as internal devices (although, again, you'll almost certainly have to install a FireWire expansion card first).

Don't play with your PC while burning a CD if you want to avoid buffer under-run.

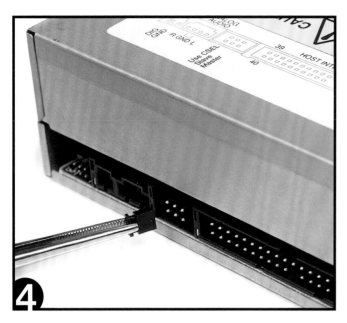

4

5

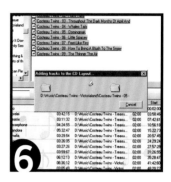

6

Before installing the new drive, check the jumper settings. If the drive is to be installed on the secondary IDE channel, as is the norm with a single CD device, these should be set to master. However, if the drive is to share a channel with the hard disk (i.e. connected to the same ribbon cable), the hard disk should be designated master and the CD drive slave. (If two drives on the same channel were both set to master or slave, neither would work). Check the documentation that came with the drive if it's not clear how to set the jumpers.

Now slide the new drive into the vacant drive bay, secure with the screws you removed earlier and connect the power, ribbon and audio cable exactly as they were connected to the original drive. Be certain to match the colour-coded strip on the cable with 'pin 1' on the drive. Carefully put everything back together, take that familiar deep breath, and switch on.

Your new drive should now work immediately without any need for special driver software. However, this is the time to install and experiment with any application software that came with the drive, as without it you can't start recording. Well, unless you have Windows XP, that is.

Buffer stuff If a PC fails to supply data to the drive quickly enough during a recording process, the drive temporarily runs out of work. Unfortunately, instead of pausing and waiting for the system to catch up, it throws out a ruined disc (= an expensive silver drinks coaster). It's a problem known as buffer under-run and it's a mighty pain in the posterior. To help alleviate it, drives come with built-in buffers. Look for at least 2 or 4MB. Better still, the latest generation of recordable drives carry a 'burnproof' tag (the 'burn' bit stems confusingly from buffer under-run) which means that a drive can start recording precisely where it left off in the case of interruption. Get one if you can.

TROUBLE-SHOOTER

If your new drive refuses to play an audio CD – and your old one worked just fine – check that the audio cable is correctly connected. It's a fiddly little plug that can easily be missed.
Any new recordable CD drive will come with *some* recording software but typically only the minimum required for rudimentary data backups. To record audio CDs or fill CDs with data piecemeal (packet writing), you may have to purchase a specialist program or two. Roxio (http://www.roxio.com) and Ahead Software (http://www.nero.com) are leading manufacturers.
If repeated buffer under-run threatens your sanity and you have more coasters than cups, try getting the drive to record at less than its top speed. This usually solves the problem. Also leave the PC well alone while it's busy recording. Doing anything else at the same time drains memory and increases the likelihood of under-run.

PART 3

Adding a DVD drive

The first D stands for Digital, the second for Disc, and the V for Video, Versatile or nothing in particular, depending who you ask. DVD is essentially another form of optical storage. The discs look just like any old CDs but with one big difference: vastly increased capacity, anywhere from 4.7GB to 17GB, to be precise – and, yes, that means that a single disc quite possibly holds more data than your current hard disk. The popularity of DVD is mainly due to the fact that a single disc can store and play a full-length feature film at a remarkably high quality level. Some weighty software programs, particularly reference titles crammed with film and sound clips, are also distributed on DVD.

What's more, a DVD-ROM drive (ROM as in read-only memory i.e. no recording ability) can also play CD-ROM, CD-R and CD-RW discs. Some very clever 'combo' DVD drives even combine the recording functionality of a CD-RW drive with DVD playback. In the name of making life as simple as possible, our ever-present mantra, such a drive is the best upgrade of all. Why fuss with separate CD-ROM, CD-RW and DVD drives when a single device does the lot?

A DVD drive turns your PC into a home cinema.

Large software programs are sometimes distributed in DVD format for convenience.

What you need to know

There are several critical considerations before you splash out on DVD.

Speed DVD drives are rated in terms of how quickly they spin, just like CD drives. However, while higher spin rates (e.g. 16x) make for quicker data transfer when installing software, all movies play at 1x, so speed is not much of an issue.

Interface Internal DVD drives use either the IDE/ATAPI or SCSI interface. Installing one is almost as straightforward as fitting a recordable CD drive. However...

Hardware acceleration Playing DVD movies on a computer demands a great deal in the way of system resources, and only a mid-range Pentium II processor or better is up to the task. This is because the video on a disc is considerably compressed and must be decompressed by the computer during playback. If the processor lags behind, the result is a jerky picture or outright failure. But all is not lost as it's possible to install a dedicated DVD decoder expansion card to take the burden away from the system processor, with the result that even humble Pentium systems can play jitter-free films. The decoder card uses a PCI slot on the motherboard (see p.72) and thus involves a little more surgery than fitting a drive alone. However, DVD playback capability is also now built in to modern graphics cards. Such cards take much of the processing strain away from the system processor and largely eliminate the need for a separate decoder card even when paired with a relatively slow processor.

Sound A good sound card is also desirable to make the most of the high quality digital audio signal used in DVD films.

Software You'll also need to install playback software to watch a movie on your monitor but something suitable may come in the box with the drive. If not, there are plenty of programs to choose from.

Don't forget to install a software player if you want to watch movies on your computer.

Upgrading to DVD

The process is essentially the same as installing a recordable CD drive (see p.60). You might choose to replace the existing CD-ROM drive or you might already have installed a CD-RW drive and now want a DVD drive to complete your system.

In the latter case, the procedure is still identical except that the new device requires a free 5.25 inch drive bay and it will certainly have to share an IDE channel with another device. If possible, connect the DVD drive to the same channel as the CD-RW drive rather than the hard disk. Set the jumpers to slave if it shares a channel or to master if the DVD is the only device on the channel.

As discussed previously, you'll either have to install a separate decoder card if you're installing the drive in a pre-Pentium II system or, better, pair it with a DVD-capable graphics card. We cover the general procedure for fitting expansion cards on p.76.

A DVD-capable graphics card is essential for jitter-free playback

Regional coding
It's a drag but DVD movies are cobbled with 'regional coding', a copyright protection measure which means that discs designed for distribution in one region do not play in drives built for other regions. In other words, only buy a disc that matches the coding of your drive. The current regions are as follows:

Code	Region
1	USA & Canada
2	Europe & Japan
3	South East Asia
4	Latin America & Australia
5	Russia, Africa and rest of Asia
6	China

Recordable DVD

If there is one certainty in computer evolution, it is this: recordable DVD drives will soon become commonplace. This means that we'll all be able to store anywhere between 4.7 and 17GB of data (and quite possibly more) on a single blank disc, just as we can now with 700MB of data using a CD-R or RW drive. But not quite yet. Why?

The problem is not unfamiliar. There are, sad to say, several competing technologies battling it out for market dominance. It's all a bit chicken and egg, really: recordable DVD won't appeal to the mass market until it's affordable, easy to use, reliable and broadly compatible (i.e. friends and colleagues can read your home-burned discs on their standard DVD-ROM drives); but this won't happen until one technology – and not necessarily the best one, if you recall the VHS vs. Betamax battle – forges ahead and wins backing from manufacturers.

For now, if you venture into the shops and enquire about a recordable DVD drive, you will likely find three rewriteable options on offer – DVD-RAM, DVD+RW and DVD-RW – and two one-time-only recordable options – DVD+R and DVD-R. The differences are many and significant and too perplexing to go into here. Frankly, it's a shambles. We won't even mention HD-DVD (High Definition-DVD) or DVD Audio (a sound-only format).

We will, however, offer two comments:

If your pockets are deep, you really need a large-scale storage solution right now and you have no need to share your recorded discs with anybody else, then it doesn't matter one jot which format you choose. Any DVD rewriteable drive will work just fine on your PC so long as you feed it compatible media. If you twisted our arms and asked which format is likely to win out, we would (very) tentatively back DVD+RW.

If, however, you can wait for a year or two, the market will undoubtedly settle down, mass production will kick in, and prices will tumble.

For more on recordable DVD, check out **http://www.dvdforum.org** and **http://www.dvdrw.com**.

Recordable DVD is already a reality but the smart money says wait for standards to settle down

TROUBLE-SHOOTER

As with installing a new CD drive, you are unlikely to run into hardware problems so long as both the BIOS (see p.153) and device are plug and play and you connect all the cables correctly.

By far the most common complaint is poor quality playback when watching a DVD movie, and this is almost always because the computer's resources are overstretched. You really don't want to be writing a novel, surfing the web, sending email and

checking your accounts while a movie is playing, so close down all other programs for the duration of the movie.

DVD playback software can also be problematic. In particular, not all programs support all audio formats. To learn more about this still emerging technology, try these sites:
http://www.pctechguide.com/10dvd.htm
http://www.intervideo.com
http://www.gocyberlink.com

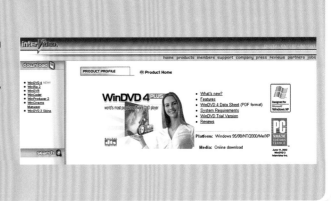

PART **3**

Step-by-step floppy drive replacement

Ah, the good old floppy drive. Slow as a sloth and capable of storing a paltry 1.44MB of data per disk, it's still a staple component in virtually every PC. The drive isn't something that you'll *upgrade* as such – there's only one standard and it's not getting any better or faster – but just occasionally a drive may call it a day and need replacing. You may be tempted not to bother, figuring that you use the thing so rarely that it's not worth the bother, but a quick re-read of p.24 should help change your mind. Should Windows go all peculiar, the first place you'll turn to is your startup disk – which, without a working drive to read it, is about as useful as a chocolate teapot.

Before *attempting any internal work on your PC, re-read the safety precautions on p.33.*

What you need to know

In truth, there's little we need to say about the floppy drive other than that it uses a 3.5 inch drive bay, has its very own dedicated channel on the motherboard, and costs next to nothing these days. So let's skip straight to an installation.

The much-maligned floppy drive is still an essential in most computer systems.

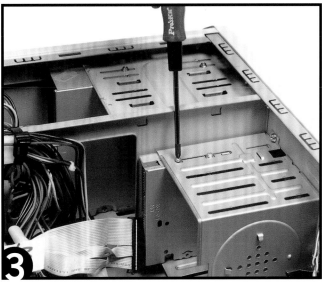

The existing floppy drive is wired up to a power supply and a ribbon cable (connected to the floppy drive controller on the motherboard, usually close to but always distinct from the IDE controllers). Note the peculiar split and twist in the cable. This dictates which device is designated as drive letter A:. Unplug the cables from the drive (not the motherboard) but keep the connectors within easy reach. You'll need them all again in a moment. Note that the power connector is smaller than the one used to wire up the CD drive.

The drive is secured in the bay with four short screws, two on either side. Remove these and set aside, and slide the drive forward until it's free. Occasionally, a 3.5 inch drive may be installed in a 5.25 inch bay, in which case there will be a mounting mechanism of some description. Make sure you can replicate the procedure with your new device.

 TECHIE CORNER

One alternative you might consider is an LS-120 SuperDisk drive: basically, an improved, proprietary version of the floppy drive that uses 120MB disks *and* reads standard floppies into the bargain. However, this device must be installed on an IDE channel just like a hard disk or a CD drive, which limits further your expansion possibilities. There can also be problems getting BIOS to recognise the drive as bootable. For full product details, see: **http://www.imation.com.**

Slide the drive in position in its bay and connect the power and ribbon cables exactly as they were connected to the original drive.

Put everything back together again, restart the system, pop a floppy disk in the drive and make sure that Windows can read from it. You might also like to reboot with your startup disk (see p.24) in the drive just to be certain that the drive works properly in an emergency.

PART ③ External drives

We've looked in detail at hard disk, CD and floppy drives, and pretty much any internal drive can be installed in exactly the same way. A tape drive for commercial backups is one popular option; a Zip or Jaz drive for low-cost, flexible, removable storage is another. The limiting factor is really the IDE controllers on the motherboard. Four devices – including the hard disk but excluding the floppy drive – are usually as far as you can go without resorting to high-tech trickery or installing an additional adaptor. Only the most recent PCs extend support to a four channels/eight drive configuration.

Pros and cons

However, in every case it's just as possible to plump for an *external* drive. True, these are always a little more expensive as you pay for a protective case, a button or two and perhaps a panel of blinking lights (for which read: external drives are something of a rip-off), but the advantages are considerable:

An external drive is portable, which means you can use it at home and in the office *and* hook it up to just about any PC anywhere. This is especially true of the latest 'hot-swappable' USB and FireWire devices which are operational almost as soon as you plug them in.

Because they simply plug into a port around the back of your PC, or perhaps into a USB hub incorporated within the monitor housing or built into the keyboard, external drives are easier to install (not that installing an internal drive is any great drama, as we hope to have demonstrated).

It's always easier to find what's wrong with a device when you can see it (and give it a shake), especially if it has self-diagnostics measures built in. And it's *much* easier to take back to the shop if it's a DOA dud.

As for the disadvantages... well, external drives need their own power source (or, sometimes, batteries), they take up room on a desk, you may have to get devices to share the same port, they're slower than their internal counterparts, and then there's that price premium we mentioned. Oh, and they're more prone to coffee spillages.

External drives offer unlimited upgrade options without the need for surgery. What's more, you can take the devices from PC to PC and use them anywhere.

PART **4** Expansion cards

After decades of hardware evolution, today's PC has emerged with a plethora of different standards and interfaces, counter-intuitive design standards and an acronym soup of a language that purports to make 'sense' of it all. But not to worry: upgrading an expansion card remains one of the most effective ways to revamp a crusty old computer. It's easy when you know how – so let's go find out.

PART **4** A word about architecture

Today's motherboards combine historical standards with the latest and fastest interfaces.

As we have seen, the motherboard is the central component in your PC system, so much so that everything else connects to it one way or another. An interface is simply a gateway through which any two components or devices can 'talk' to each other. We've looked already at how internal drives use the IDE interface, talked about slots and sockets for processors, and plugged extra memory straight into the motherboard. Now let's turn to expansion cards.

Get slotted

Expansion slots are connectors on a motherboard used for attaching printed circuit boards (cards). The beauty of such a system is that you can immeasurably improve the performance of your computer without wielding a soldering iron. There are three main expansion slot standards (in order of age):

ISA (Industry Standard Architecture). ISA slots are black, long, slow and all but obsolete. You're most likely to find a modem in one. Or dust. Expect to find a couple inside the case in all but the most modern PCs – they are currently being phased out by manufacturers.

PCI (Peripheral Component Interconnect). The PCI standard is faster than ISA and its slots (white, short) typically host sound cards, older graphics cards and perhaps a DVD decoder. A USB or SCSI controller can also be bolted on through the PCI interface to give a computer still more interface options. Three slots is an acceptable minimum, four better, and more are always welcome.

AGP (Accelerated Graphics Port). This is a slot designed exclusively for modern graphics cards, specifically optimised for 3-dimensional effects and digital video. There is only ever one AGP slot per motherboard, and you'll only find it on Pentium II systems and above. However, a modern machine is no cast-iron guarantee of AGP as some motherboards incorporate the necessary graphics chips directly within the motherboard itself.

Blank check

Expansion slots are positioned on the motherboard in such a way that one end of an installed card pokes through the PC's rear panel. Flick back to p.17 and note how the graphics connector (a plug for the monitor) and the audio connector (a plug for speakers) are accessible externally. Or just peek around the back of your computer to see the visible end of your installed cards. The holes that afford expansion cards access to the outside world are usually covered with metal blanking plates but these can be easily removed.

One factor to watch: it's not uncommon for adjacent PCI and ISA slots to share a blanking plate, with the implication that you can install one or the other type of card but not both simultaneously. Newer motherboards may also have an AMR (Audio Modem Riser) or CNR (Communications and Networking Riser) slot which also encroaches on the array of blanking plates.

Blanking plates can be removed to open up access to expansion slots.

Integration

Back on p.15, we mentioned that some motherboards incorporate a variety of features within their own circuitry, specifically graphical and sound output and sometimes a modem or network card. The alleged attractions of such an approach are price (it's cheaper to build and buy a PC with an 'integrated' motherboard than one bustling with expansion cards) and ease of use (because there's no way to upgrade these features, the hapless PC owner has no need to open the lid and poke around inside). Now you may consider that intentionally making upgrades difficult, is a peculiar approach. Certainly, we are not inclined to recommend an integrated system unless you're quite sure that you won't want to upgrade your computer a year or two down the line (it's a bold buyer who would make such a claim) or you're buying a basic office-based system as opposed to a funky, multifunctional, all-singing, all-dancing affair for the home.

Let's now look in some detail at three popular and worthwhile expansion card upgrades.

Integrated circuitry is fine and dandy but it makes later upgrades trickier.

TECHIE CORNER

Bits and buses The physical path between any two computer components – in other words, the wires that make the connection – is called a bus. The size, or width, of the bus is a measure of how much data it can handle at any one time. The ISA standard is based on a 16-bit bus, which means that it transfers a maximum of 16 bits of data per processor cycle (a bit being the smallest binary unit i.e. a single 1 or 0). PCI is a 32-bit standard and is thus capable of twice the workload within the same time. When we say that one interface is 'faster' than another, this is simply shorthand for saying that it's capable of sustaining a higher rate of data transfer. Although AGP is also 32-bits wide, it operates at twice the speed of PCI (66MHz rather than 33MHz) and is thus better suited to the high demands of graphics cards where a great deal of data has to be processed as quickly as possible to keep video and games in full flow.

For (much) more on AGP, look here: **http://developer.intel.com/ technology/agp**

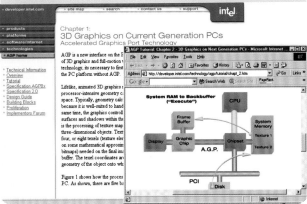

PART 4 Upgrading your graphics card

Perhaps you want to edit digital video footage on your PC. Maybe you'd like to add a TV tuner card and use it as a television. If you've developed an interest in photography, your old graphics card may be unable to display your digital snapshots in all their glory. In all these cases and more, a graphics card upgrade is likely to be a good investment.

But one word of caution: if you intend to turn your PC into a games machine then yes, you'll need a state of the art graphics card – but you'll *also* need a fast processor, bags of RAM, a reasonable sound card, probably a joystick, a decent monitor and stacks of free hard disk space. In many – nay, most – cases, a standalone games console may be a better bet. Indeed, a console *plus* a new portable television can cost less than the hardware upgrades you'll need to transform a basic PC.

That said, the popularity of computer games has been directly responsible for some remarkable technological advances, and you will certainly be impressed with the performance of the latest graphics hardware if your experience of gaming begins and ends with Solitaire.

Resolving resolution Your PC's graphics card and monitor are inextricably entwined. The monitor displays the picture but the picture itself is generated by the graphics card (also called the video card or board). For best results, you want the card and the monitor working together to mutual advantage.

Consider the question of resolution: a measure of how much detail you see on screen. A resolution of 800 x 600 (a standard known as SVGA, or Super Video Graphics Array) means that an image is composed of 600 rows of 800 pixels (tiny points of light). A higher resolution like 1280 x 1024 equates to many more pixels, and that in turn means that more images can be squeezed onto the screen without loss of detail. The images do, however, get smaller.

Now, graphics cards usually support many different resolutions but there is a physical limit on any given monitor's maximum display. What it boils down to is this: if you have a 15 inch monitor and don't plan to replace it any time soon, a basic graphics card that supports a resolution of 800 x 600 is all you really need. By contrast, low resolution is wasted on a 21 inch monster monitor; you'll be far more satisfied with a 1600 x 1200 display.

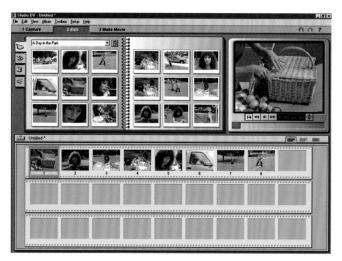

Solitaire won't strain your graphics card but digital video might.

Here are the recommended optimum display settings

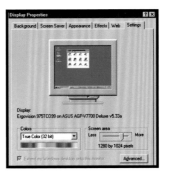

*Screen size **15 inch**
Resolution **800 x 600***

*Screen size **17 inch**
Resolution **1024 x 768***

*Screen size **19 inch**
Resolution **1280 x 1024***

*Screen size **21 inch**
Resolution **1600 x 1200***

What you need to know

Graphics cards are plagued with technical specifications and you need to understand at least the basics in order to make an informed purchase.

Interface As discussed earlier, graphics cards use either a PCI or an AGP slot. The big advantage of AGP is that the card can access main system RAM quickly, which avoids bottlenecks and boosts performance. It would be very unusual to find an AGP-equipped motherboard with a PCI graphics card installed, but in such circumstances you would certainly want to upgrade to AGP. Curiously, for reasons that we'll come to in the monitor section, you might want to leave an old PCI card in place whilst upgrading to AGP; similarly, adding a PCI card alongside an AGP card would count as an upgrade (we're talking about running a dual monitor setup, in case you can't contain your excitement). But in most cases you'll swap one AGP or PCI card for another of the same type.

Memory Graphics cards come with their own slice of memory onboard. How much dictates just what it can do, and how quickly. Memory also determines how many colours the card can display. If you right-click on the Windows Desktop, select Properties and click on the Settings tab, you'll see your current card's colour setting. If you now try to increase the setting – say, from 256 to 65,000 (16-bit) – you may find that the resolution slider automatically adjusts to a lower setting. This is because cards can typically pump out a full colour range at a low resolution *or* a high resolution in fewer colours, but not both simultaneously.

Memory matters. The minimum a modern graphics card offers, typically 4MB, will get you to 1280 x 1024 resolution in 24-bit colour, and that is just fine for business work. However, you'll need 64MB or more for today's computer games.

TECHIE CORNER

Games standards
Stick a CD or cartridge in a games console and it'll play first time, *every* time. Not necessarily so with PC games. The trouble is that games are usually developed around one particular software standard (or API – Application Programming Interface) and not all graphics cards support all standards. The best bet is to buy only games that are compatible with your card or, if you're upgrading your graphics card now and already have a collection of games, plump for one that definitely supports your favourites. The sands of 3-D standards are ever shifting but names to look for are Direct3D and OpenGL.
For a comprehensive guide to gaming standards, look here:
http://www.pctechguide.com/05 graph2.htm

Today's graphics cards use the AGP slot and come with their own memory chips.

Step-by-step graphics card upgrade

The beauty of expansion slot architecture is that internal cards can be installed and uninstalled with virtually no effort. Here we replace an AGP graphics card with another.

Before *attempting any internal work on your PC, re-read the safety precautions on p.31. Be sure to ground yourself and wear your antistatic wrist-strap, as expansion cards are very susceptible to static charges. Keep your new card in its antistatic bag until the last moment.*

A single *screw secures the graphics card to the chassis. Remove this now and set aside.*

Carefully *remove the old graphics card from its slot. You may find retaining clips that must be removed. Hold the card by the edges and be sure not to damage its components with your fingers. This can be a fiddly business, particularly if there are other expansion cards either side, and it might take a little effort to get the card free. Do not rock it from side to side.*

...and more of what you need to know

Processor Yes, graphics cards also have processors. As you would expect, the faster the processor, the better the card is at rendering complex graphics. Look for the term 'graphics accelerator' or, for the ultimate hardware high, a GPU (Graphics Processing Unit). Cooling fans are now commonplace.

Dimensions In ye olden days, graphics cards were two dimensional affairs, perfectly adequate for office-style work but hopeless for playing games or displaying digital video. Then along came 3-D graphics cards that sat in a slot alongside the existing 2-D model and kicked in when intensive video rendering was called for. This was clearly a daft set of affairs and so, in time, evolved the next generation of cards that combined 2- and 3-D functions. Badly. Some time thereafter, *good* combo cards emerged, and that's where we are today. Incidentally, 3-D isn't really three dimensional; it's just clever trickery that adds the illusion of depth to video presentations.

External connectors Before buying any new graphics card, consider carefully just what you want it to do. If its sole responsibility is to work with your PC monitor, no problem: any card will do that. But if you want to watch games or DVD movies on a TV screen, an S-Video output would be useful. Some cards are equipped with video-in connectors so you can capture video from a camcorder or VHS recorder, and you might even find a connector for 3-D glasses (be prepared to be ridiculed by your family and friends). One further consideration; if you intend to connect a *digital* LCD monitor to your computer, look for a graphics card with a DVI (Digital Visual Interface) connector. More on this when we look at monitor upgrade on p90.

More on this when we look at monitor upgrade on p90.

TROUBLE-SHOOTER

Never upgrade a graphics card and a monitor simultaneously. From a diagnostic point of view, you only want to work with one suspect device at a time. If Windows will only start in safe mode, the card's refresh rate is probably set too high for the monitor. Lower the setting in Display Properties. Click Start, Control Panel and Display, and look in the Adaptor tab. Your monitor probably has its own display settings, usually accessible through buttons on its casing, and you may wish to adjust the brightness or contrast to optimise the display. You can also adjust the image size to suit the viewable screen area.

Take the new card from its antistatic bag and gently insert it in the vacant AGP slot, making sure to match its connecting edge precisely with the slot opening. Again, be sure not to touch the card's components. If necessary, use a gentle end-to-end rocking motion to ease it into the slot.

Now secure the card to the chassis using the screw that you removed earlier. Also reattach any retaining clips, if possible.

Carefully put everything back together, reconnect the monitor cable, and switch on the PC. All being well, Windows will detect the new card, launch the New Hardware Found wizard and prompt you for the appropriate drivers. Have any CD or floppy disks that came with the drive to hand along with your Windows installation disc and follow the instructions. Alternatively, you may have to manually install the driver by running a setup program from the supplied disc. It's impossible to be definitive here as procedures vary, but the manual should make clear what to do.

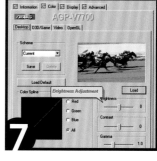

As well as a driver to get the PC and the monitor talking to each other, your new graphics card may well come with additional software tools and toys, including games demos, a DVD player, utilities for adjusting display settings, an electronic manual and goodness knows what else. We'd suggest installing everything to start with and removing any bits and pieces you don't fancy.

 TECHIE CORNER

Display settings Changing the display settings *before* upgrading your graphics card can help to avert problems with Windows. If the new card's manual says something along the line of: 'change your display driver to Standard VGA', proceed as follows (note: the precise wording may vary)

1 Click Start, point to Settings, click Control Panel, and then double-click Display.
2 Click the Settings tab, and then click Advanced.
3 Click the Adaptor tab, and then click Change.
4 Click Next, click "Display a list of all the drivers in a specific location so you can select the driver you want," then click Next.
5 Click Show All Devices.
6 In the Manufacturers box, click (Standard Display Types).
7 In the Models box, click Standard Display Adaptor (VGA), click OK, and then click Next.

8 Click Next, click Next, and then click Finish.
9 Click Close, click Close again, and then click Yes to restart your computer.

NB: The above instructions are adapted from Microsoft's Knowledge Base on the web and used with permission. For more information, look here:
http://support.microsoft.com/ default.aspx?scid-kb;EN-US;q127139
An alternative approach is to uninstall the original card's drivers through the Add/Remove Programs utility (see p.126) just before switching off the PC and installing the new card.

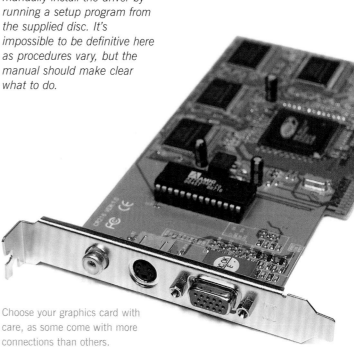

Choose your graphics card with care, as some come with more connections than others.

PART 4 Upgrading your sound card

Time was when the average desktop PC emitted only feeble and occasional bleeps. But these days even the humblest domestic computer is a veritable home entertainment centre. A sound card is standard equipment in any new system, as are, unfortunately, cheap, tinny speakers that do it no justice whatsoever. More of them later but for now merely note that good speakers can enhance sound quality up to a point but the sound itself is generated internally. A powerful sound card is the starting point for aural satisfaction.

With a decent sound card onboard, your PC can eclipse your stereo in the audio stakes.

Why bother? Do you really want your PC to double as a stereo? Well, yes if you want to play audio CDs on your computer. Thanks to the phenomenal popularity of the MP3 file format and the widespread distribution (and piracy) of music on the internet, you could even build and play a music collection entirely on and from your hard disk. And then there are multimedia presentations like encyclopaedias and reference titles. And DVD movie soundtracks. And computer games. And sound files on web pages. And internet-based radio and TV channels. And so on…

Moreover, a sound card means that you can record your *own* music on your computer if you have the mind and/or the talent to do such a thing. Have you considered the benefits of internet telephony where long-distance calls on the internet cost a fraction of normal telephone charges? There's also the evolving world of voice recognition: speak into a microphone and smart software transcribes your words onto the page as text.

All of these examples require a sound card. The good news is that your PC almost certainly has one onboard already; the better news is that the quality and flexibility of sound technology has appreciated dramatically these past few years, yet even top of the range hardware is realistically priced. So, if your card is found wanting, give it the heave and slot in a new one.

First, of course, and as always, do a little research.

What you need to know

Figuring out which card best suits your needs is not too tricky if you keep an eye on the following considerations:

Interface Modern sound cards all use the PCI (32-bit) expansion slot. There's every possibility that your existing card is sited in an ISA (16-bit) slot but it's time to bid it a fond farewell.

Multi-channel audio Cinema goers will be well aware of the three-dimensional 'surround sound' techniques used in today's movies, where the audio comes at you from all angles, but you might be surprised to learn that you can achieve similar effects at home with a suitable sound card, especially when playing DVD movies on your computer. You'll need a whole bunch of speakers for the full effect (see p.100) but there's nothing quite like it for realism. If you're serious about your sound, read and absorb this sites: **http://www.dolby.custhelp.com**

Modern sound cards use the more powerful PCI interface.

MIDI – or Musical Instrument Digital Interface – is as the name suggests an interface that enables a musical instrument (typically a keyboard) to connect to the sound card in order to play and record music. The technology is also widely used in computer games so a MIDI-capable card is a must.

Wave table (WAV) A wave table card (see Techie Corner overleaf) is essential for audio fidelity. The quality of a card's sound is measured in terms of bits, where more is better. Go for a 64-bit card if you intend to record your own music or are prepared to invest in speakers that make the most of the card's superior output; otherwise, a 32-bit card will suffice.

Duplex means that a sound card can make and record sounds simultaneously. Most conversations are duplex to some degree – we talk and listen at the same time – so a full duplex card is essential for PC chat and telephony.

A PC can be a full-blown audio entertainment centre when fitted out with the latest sound card kit

External connectors Important connectors include audio output (for speakers), audio input for recording from an external devices like microphones or MIDI keyboards.

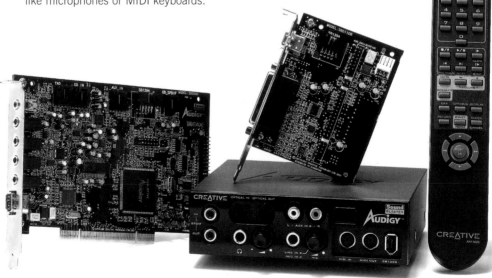

PART **4** Step-by-step sound card upgrade

Upgrading a sound card is just as straightforward as replacing a graphics card. In this example, we'll remove the original card from its ISA slot and install a new PCI card.

Before attempting any internal work on your PC, re-read the safety precautions on p.31. Be sure to ground yourself and wear your antistatic wrist-strap, as expansion cards are very susceptible to static charges. Keep your new card in its antistatic bag until the last moment.

Note the thin audio cable connecting the sound card to the CD-ROM (or CD-RW) drive. Carefully unplug this at the sound card end only.

A single screw secures the sound card to the chassis. Remove this now and set aside.

TECHIE CORNER

Sampling Way back yonder, sound cards used a technology called FM (Frequency Modulation) Synthesis whereby the tone of, say, a violin was generated according to complex mathematical formulae. This worked just fine as far as it went but you'd never be fooled into thinking a Grapelli was in the room. A radically different technology called wave table synthesis was then developed. Here, actual recordings – *samples* – of musical instruments are digitised, stored in memory and called upon to reproduce truly lifelike music. It's still synthetic, of course, but it's the next best thing to housing a miniaturised orchestra in your PC.

Carefully remove the old sound card from its ISA slot. Hold the card by the edges and be sure not to damage its components with your fingers. This can be a fiddly business, particularly if there are other expansion cards either side, and it might take a little effort to get the card free. Do not rock it from side to side.

Take the new card from its antistatic bag and position it gently on but not in a free PCI slot. This is just to check which metal blanking plate on the chassis needs to be removed in order that the card can access the outside world.

Replace the card in its bag while you remove both the retaining screw and the blanking plate.

7

8

Gently insert the new card in the PCI slot, making sure to match its connecting edge precisely with the slot opening. Again, be sure not to touch the card's components. If necessary, use a gentle end-to-end rocking motion to ease it into the slot.

Now secure the card to the chassis using the screw that held the blanking plate in place or one that came with the drive. You may also care to close up the ISA slot's hole with the blanking plate. Anything that keeps the dust down is good.

9

Attach the audio cable to the appropriate connector on the card (consult the manual for directions). In the unlikely event that the plug on the audio cable doesn't fit your new card's connector – a sign of changing standards – use the cable supplied in the box (assuming that there is such a thing). You will of course have to connect it to both the sound card and the CD drive. Carefully put everything back together, reconnect the speakers, and switch on the PC. All being well, Windows will detect the new card, launch the New Hardware Found wizard and prompt you for the appropriate drivers. Have any CD or floppy disks that came with the card to hand along with your Windows installation disc and follow the instructions.

TROUBLE-SHOOTER

Never upgrade a sound card and speakers simultaneously! From a diagnostic point of view, you only want to work with one suspect device at a time.

No sound when you play an audio CD? Did the speakers work just fine with the old card? Try plugging headphones into the CD-ROM drive (there should be a jack on the front) to make sure that both the drive and your CD playback software are working. If so, and if you have a suitable cable with 3.5mm jacks on either end (see p158), connect the headphone socket to the audio *input* on the sound card. If you can hear the CD through the speakers

now, the problem lies with the internal audio cable. Open the PC (after taking all the usual precautions) and ensure that it's correctly connected at both ends. Replace if necessary.

Just on the off-chance, double-click the speaker icon in the System Tray (the right hand end of the

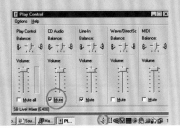

Windows Taskbar) and make sure that the CD drive has not been muted.

Also try playing audio files saved on the hard disk. If necessary, use the Windows Find Files tool to seek out files with the extension WAV, WMA or MP3.

Have a look in Device Manager (see p.22) and ensure that the sound card icon is not flagged with an exclamation or question mark (this would indicate a problem or conflict).

Modern sound card software is often fiendishly complex. There will likely be a host of settings to play around with, probably some

diagnostic tools too, and almost certainly much less help in the manual than you would like. Look for an electronic manual on the supplied CD-ROM or consult the card manufacturer's website for further help.

PART 4 Upgrading your modem

Modems are now a standard computer accessory. In fact, you quite possibly bought a computer in the first place precisely *because* it had a modem onboard. There may be cheaper, more convenient and in many ways better ways to get online, but the PC still provides the most common route into cyberspace.

If your current system does not have a modem, there are plenty of reasons to add one: to access email, the world wide web, newsgroups, bulletin boards and all the other areas of the internet; to send and receive (paperless) faxes; to set up your computer as a basic telephone answering machine or an advanced voicemail system. But there's only one good reason to *upgrade* a modem, apart from hardware failure, and that's to take advantage of the latest standards.

Ins and outs Although most new computers have modems fitted internally, we would strongly suggest that you consider purchasing an external modem this time around. Yes, they are slightly more expensive (although probably not as much as you'd expect) but they have several distinct advantages over their internal expansion card counterparts. Namely:

Diagnostics All external modems have an array of blinking lights that reveal what it's up to at any precise moment e.g. sending a fax or downloading a file from the internet. This makes it much easier to diagnose problems. Indeed, simply switching a modem off and back on again resolves many a headache. Just try doing *that* with an internal model.

Installation External modems use either a serial or a USB port. These are real, physical connections that leave little room for doubt. Internal modems, by contrast, generally sit in either an ISA or a PCI slot but use a kind of virtual port known to Windows as COM 3 or COM 4. Installing drivers and resolving problems can prove troublesome.

Convenience An external modem leaves an internal expansion slot free for another device. Remember, you only have so many slots to go around.

Modems come in all shapes and sizes but it's speed that really counts.

Where would we be without the wonders of the world wide web?

The right software can turn your PC into a communications centre.

What you need to know

A glance at the specification sheet of a standard modem would send you to sleep in an instant. We're going to ignore the intricacies of error correction, data compression, protocols and parity because it's immensely dull and irrelevant in the current context. Here instead are the essentials:

Speed Measured in bits per second (bps). An analogue modem downloads data at a maximum rate of 56,000bps, which is why so many of us spend so much time waiting for web pages to load in our browsers. For a while, two competing 56,000bps standards called K56Flex and X2 slugged it out but neither secured total market domination and eventually they came together under the banner of V.90 standard. This has now been superseded by the marginally improved V.92, and that's what to look for in the specs.

If your PC has a slower 28,800 or 33,600bps modem, you should see some improvement from an upgrade to V.92. Web pages will appear more quickly and large emails won't take quite so long to download.

Fax A fax modem copies or *emulates* the workings of a standard fax machine (which is, after all, just another device that sends analogue data through the telephone line). This means that you can prepare a letter in your word processor program and fax it anywhere in the world without having to print it out and feed it through a standalone fax machine. Almost but not quite all modems can do this: look for the word fax on the box or a standard called CCITT Group 3 Fax.

Voice A voice-enabled modem works just like an answering machine – it intercepts incoming calls, plays a recorded greeting

TECHIE CORNER

Broadband If ever a technology was in a state of flux, broadband internet access is it. Depending on where you live in the world and how much you're prepared to pay, cable or DSL (Digital Subscriber Line) connections may or may not be available in your area. These typically offer download speeds 10 times and upwards that of a humble modem. The dream is that one day everybody will have an always-on, affordable, fast internet connection (remember the 'information superhighway'?) But we're not there yet. Not by a long shot. To learn more about the different routes online, start here:
http://www.dslforum.org
http://www.zdnet.co.uk/news/
specials/2001/04/broadband/
whatbroadband.html

What's in a name? Modem is an acronym for modulator/demodulator. In a nutshell, a modem converts the digital language of computers into a series of beeps and whistles that can be sent down a telephone line and converted back into digital data by a modem at the other end of the line. Typically, the other modem belongs to an Internet Service Provider which then connects you to the internet at large. Hence you get to surf the web and send email through your telephone line. It's all terribly clever – but not, unfortunately, terribly swift.

and lets callers leave messages – but with the right software you can also set up and manage a complex voicemail service. Usually, the computer must be switched on and connected to the phone line for this to work, but some *external* modems are smart enough to answer the phone and take messages all by themselves.

Software Modems rely on application software to do their thing. All that you need to access the internet is built into Windows but 'communications software' is designed specifically to handle fax and voice functions. Any new modem should come with at least a basic communications package in the box.

So, in summary, if you want a good modem look for V.90, fax and voice. And if you want an easy life, plump for an external model.

Installing your new modem The method for installing an internal modem is precisely the same as that for installing a graphics or a sound card: take all the usual precautions, plug it into a free expansion slot (either PCI or ISA, depending on the model), put everything back together again and restart your computer. At this point, the New Hardware Found wizard should appear and prompt you for the driver. Pop the supplied CD-ROM in its drive and follow the onscreen instructions.

An internal modem is neater and cheaper but an external model is portable and easier to trouble shoot.

TROUBLE-SHOOTER

Uninstall the drivers for any existing internal modem *before* installing a new modem in the same expansion slot. Go to the Device Manager tab in System properties (see p.22), highlight the modem's icon, and click Remove. Now switch off the computer, remove the old modem and install the new device. This should help ensure that Windows prompts for the new driver through the New Hardware Found wizard.

Just installed a V.92 modem and you can't connect at 56,000bps? Join the club. 56K is a theoretical speed which is seldom (okay, never) achieved in real life. This is due to various factors, including but not limited to the volume of internet traffic, the age and quality of your telephone wiring, and the mood of the gods. Connection speeds of around 40K are average and, sad to say, as good as you're likely to get without a broadband connection. **Some internal** modems have two connectors on the external faceplate: one for a cable that runs to the phone socket on the wall; and one into which a telephone extension may be

plugged. Failing this, you can buy a two-into-one adaptor for the wall socket and so connect both the modem and a telephone. You can't use both at once, of course – a live internet connection ties up the telephone line just like a regular call – but it does save fiddling around with plugs.

Most hassles are related one way or another to Dial-Up Networking, the Windows program that a modem uses to connect to an ISP. See p.134 for help with common problems.

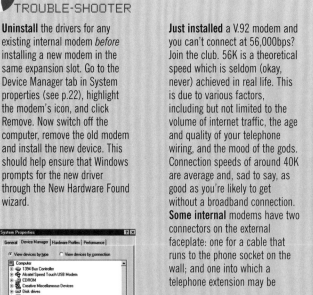

PART 4 Adding USB and Firewire

All PCs now come with at least a couple of USB (Universal Serial Bus) ports on board and some, but by no means all, have FireWire (or IEEE1394, to be precise and pedantic) capability built in, too. Both are fast interfaces ideally suited to connecting a range of external peripherals to your computer, and either can be added as a simple upgrade.

If you're wondering which interface is 'better', you're not alone. FireWire used to be much, much faster and more expensive than USB, which made it the natural choice for connecting digital video cameras to computers, but the brand new USB 2 standard is for the moment at least, even faster than FireWire. This inevitably muddies the waters. As things stand, USB is generally used for scanners, printers, keyboards, digital cameras, music players and the like. The faster USB 2 now makes it possible to hook up external hard disks and fast CD or DVD drives. FireWire is still the natural gateway for digital video – most camcorders have a FireWire connector built in – but, as FireWire-enabled devices gradually lose their premium status and drop in price, we're starting to see a wider selection of external disks and drives on the market.

If your computer already has USB ports, we'd suggest upgrading to USB 2 if and when you feel the need for greater speed. FireWire remains a must for video enthusiasts, but do bear in mind that you'll need a very fast processor and bags of RAM to successfully edit your footage.

USB offers almost unlimited expansion capabilities. Go for the newer, faster USB 2 standard.

Check that your system can use USB before you take the plunge.

You can add USB and FireWire to your computer with a single PCI expansion card. This Adaptec card has three USB and two FireWire ports.

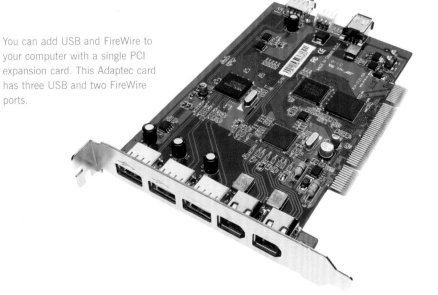

USB recently had a major speed upgrade but USB 2 is fully backwards compatible with USB 1.1.

Perhaps the best upgrade of all is installing a combined USB 2/FireWire card. These are now readily available and open up all sorts of connection possibilities in one easy, affordable move.

One small caveat: the first release of Windows 95 and everything than went before it had no support whatsoever for USB, so an operating system upgrade to at least Windows 98 or, preferably, Millennium Edition or XP is in order first. Intel has a free software utility called USBready that can give your PC a complete once over for USB readiness. Download it here: **http://www.usb.org/data/usbready.exe**

What you need to know

Speed An awful lot of data can pass through a USB or FireWire bus in a short time. The older flavour of USB (1.1) had a top speed of 1.5MB per second, but USB 2 runs at up to 60MB per second. FireWire achieves a maximum throughput of 50MB per second.

Flexibility You can connect up to 127 USB devices or 63 FireWire devices to a single port, but that's more impressive in theory than in reality. While FireWire devices can be linked together daisy-chain fashion – each new device simply plugs into the last one in the chain – USB requires the use of hubs, or expansion boxes with multiple USB ports. Many keyboards and monitors come with USB hubs built in.

Plug and play Windows will (or certainly should) recognise any USB or FireWire device as soon as it's plugged in and prompt for the drivers immediately i.e. no rebooting. No fussing with jumpers or other fiddly hardware settings either.

Hot-swappable Instead of having to reboot your PC every time you connect a device, you can plug and unplug USB and FireWire devices at will.

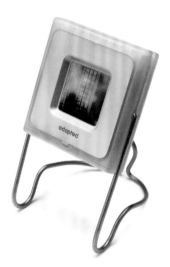

USB expansion hubs are essential if you want to connect several devices to a single port.

TECHIE CORNER

U-S-B Let's consider this acronym. 'U' is for *universal*, a reflection of the fact that a single, standardized connector and cable combination works with all USB devices. That means no more fiddling with X-to-Y-to-Z-to-whatever adaptors and odd-shaped, proprietary plugs. 'S' is for *serial*, which means that data passes through the connection one bit at a time (as opposed to *parallel*, in which several bits go through together). And 'B' is for *bus*, which is just the wiring along which data flows. So now you know.

PART 4

Step-by-step
USB card upgrade

USB controller cards typically come with two or four USB connectors and use the PCI expansion slot. Sounds simple? It is. Here's how. Note that the installation process for a FireWire card is identical

Before *attempting any internal work on your PC, re-read the safety precautions on p.31. Be sure to ground yourself and wear your antistatic wrist-strap, as expansion cards are very susceptible to static charges.*

Take *the new card from its antistatic bag and position it gently on but not in a free PCI slot. This is just to check which metal blanking plate needs to be removed.*

Replace *the card in its bag while you remove both the retaining screw and the blanking plate.*

TROUBLE-SHOOTER

There's nothing much that can go wrong providing you install the controller card correctly. However, here are a couple of things to look out for:
USB cables have different connectors on either end. The flatter, wider connector – Type A – goes to the USB port, and the squat, square Type B connector goes to the device. *Never* use a cable with Type A connectors on both ends to try to wire two

computers together. For one thing, such cables are illegal; for another, you'll blow up both PCs and burn down your house.
Don't buy a USB cable longer than 5 metres. It won't work. If you really need to cover a long distance, either add a powered hub every 5 metres or daisy-chain together up to five 'active extension' cables to boost the signal.

Take *out the new USB card again and gently insert it in the vacant PCI slot, making sure to match its connecting edge precisely with the slot opening. Be sure to hold the card carefully without touching its components. If necessary, use a gentle end-to-end rocking motion to ease it into the slot.*

Now *secure the card to the chassis using the screw that held the blanking plate in place. Carefully put everything back together and switch on the PC. All being well, Windows will detect the new card, launch the New Hardware Found wizard and prompt you for the appropriate drivers. Have any CD or floppy disks that came with the card to hand along with your Windows installation disc and follow the instructions.*

PART 5 Peripheral devices

A peripheral device is any component in a computer system that isn't actually the computer itself. If you take away the processor, memory and motherboard, all you're left with is a box of bits that falls some way short of a working PC. But the monitor, keyboard, mouse and printer are mere add-ons. So too are the hard disk, CD-ROM and floppy drive. Here we'll look at upgrading the most common external peripherals, beginning with the most important – and expensive – of them all.

Upgrading your monitor

Because monitors are so pricey, manufacturers and retailers of budget – and even high-end – computer systems tend to cut corners here first. But while a 15-inch display unit may have looked just fine in the shop, do you now find yourself shuffling the chair ever closer each day just to see what's going on? Has the picture lost some of its sparkle and colour depth? Have you taken up digital photography or computer gaming and found that your ageing monitor no longer cuts the mustard? It's time to save your eyesight and go for a bigger, better model. Choose wisely and it will serve you well for years – and, unlike the rest of your system, it won't be obsolete as soon as you get it home.

What you need to know

There are two main types of computer monitor – CRT (Cathode Ray Tube) and LCD (Liquid Crystal Display). Here's a brief summary of the pros and cons.

Screen size The screen size of a monitor is a diagonal measurement from corner to corner. However, while a 17-inch LCD model will indeed have a viewable screen of 17 inches, as you would hope and expect, the same size of CRT monitor typically offers a *viewable* screen size of only 16 inches or less.

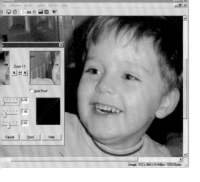

If digital photography is a hobby, you'll need a good monitor to see the results at their best.

15" LCD = 15" viewable area

17" CRT = 16" viewable area

This is because the quoted figure is a measure of the cathode ray tube itself, part of which is always hidden from view by the monitor housing. Indeed, we've seen 17-inch monitors that offer just a fraction over 15 inches of visible screen. Look for an 'actual screen area' figure, or whip out a tape measure and make your own comparisons.

Distortion Thanks to clever manufacturing techniques, CRT screens are now much flatter than they once were. This helps to reduce distortion, especially around the edges. Best of the bunch are those imaginatively called 'flat', as opposed to 'flat squared' or 'spherical' (avoid). LCD screens are perfectly flat so distortion issues don't arise.

In fact, there are several different manufacturing techniques and monitor standards. The two terms you are most likely to encounter are *shadow mask* and *aperture grill*. The first incorporates a perforated sheet of metal that focuses electron beams on to the screen, often used in FST (Flat Square Tube) models where the curvature of the glass is minimised. The second replaces the perforated sheet with a series of vertical wires through which the beams are channelled. These are held in place by two horizontal wires that can usually be seen (just), if you stare at the screen hard enough. Some people find this irritating but the aperture grill approach means that almost completely flat glass can be used to make a monitor. To find out more, look here: **http://www.iiyama.com/support2/tech.htm**

Resolution We discussed resolution on p.74, where we pointed out that the graphics card and monitor should be matched to produce the best quality picture. However, CRT monitors generally run well and look good at a full range of resolutions whereas LCD screens are optimised to work at a single resolution.

Refresh rate A measure of how many times per second the monitor redraws the image on screen. As a rule, the higher the

CRT Screen

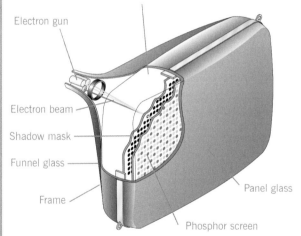

Inner magnetic shield
Electron gun
Electron beam
Shadow mask
Funnel glass
Frame
Panel glass
Phosphor screen

LCD Screen

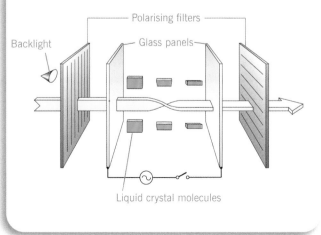

Polarising filters
Backlight
Glass panels
Liquid crystal molecules

resolution, the harder it is to maintain a high refresh rate; as another, a high refresh rate means less visible flicker, and that means no headaches or eyestrain. Look for a CRT monitor capable of sustaining a refresh rate of 85Hz at a resolution of 1024 x 768, and at least 75Hz at 1280 x 1024. (Refresh rates are not so important with LCD monitors because of the different display technology: around 60Hz is acceptable.)

Dimensions No comparison here. CRT monitors are big, bulky and heavy; LCDs are neater, much shallower and relatively lightweight. If you're pushed for space or don't fancy bashing a hole in your wall to accommodate the rear end of a CRT monitor, stretch the budget and splash out on LCD. Alternatively, consider 'short neck' CRT monitors where a premium price buys a much reduced tube depth.

Viewing angle CRT screens can be viewed from just about any angle – try it and see – but you need to be sitting pretty straight on to an LCD monitor to see the full picture. Not a big issue, perhaps, and the viewing angles are improving all the time, but LCDs are not ideally suited to communal use. Then again, does your family really sit around the PC on a regular basis?

Price LCD monitors used to be *much* more expensive than CRTs but mass production has brought the prices tumbling down and now they are pretty much standard equipment with new PCs. Also, when you're making comparisons, remember that a 15-inch LCD offers practically the same visible viewing area as the average 17-inch CRT.

There's no getting away from it: LCD monitors are infinitely sleeker and sexier than their CRT cousins.

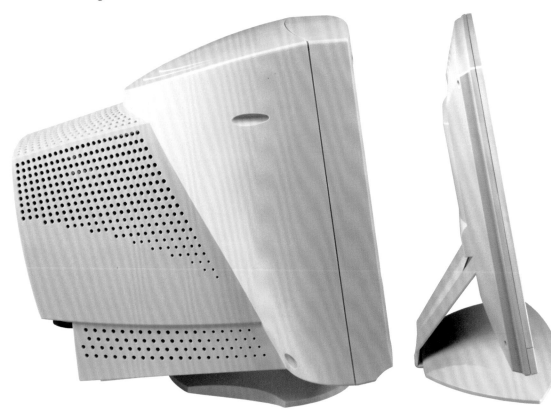

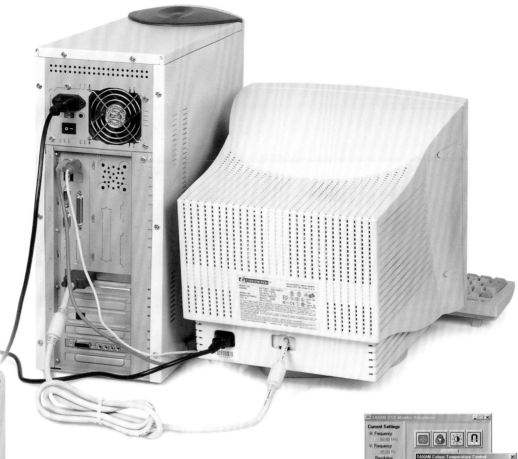

![TROUBLE-SHOOTER]

TROUBLE-SHOOTER

No picture? It sounds obvious but make sure that the monitor is plugged in *and* switched on.
Also check that the graphics card isn't trying to produce an image at a higher resolution and/or refresh rate than the monitor can handle.
Is the brightness set to zero? It sounds unlikely but it can happen during experimentation with the monitor's own controls.
Failing that, reconnect your original monitor and see if the picture returns. If so, it's a safe bet that your new monitor is a dud – but do seek out the troubleshooting section in the manual and eliminate all possible problems before sending it back.
Dead pixels It's a fact of life that virtually every LCD monitor sold comes with a dead pixel or two. These look like tiny black or red dots on the screen through which no light or image appears. However, unless your screen is peppered with them to the extent that it detracts from normal use – a rare occurrence indeed – don't worry about it.

Installing your new monitor

On one hand, this is a simple case of switching off your PC, unplugging the old monitor, plugging in the new one, and rebooting. Windows then detects that something has changed and launches the New Hardware Found wizard, at which point you'll be prompted to install the monitor's driver. But (you just knew there would be a but), it takes a little more effort to get a perfect picture.

Get tweaking First off, you'll want to experiment with the monitor's own controls. Modern monitors typically have a couple of buttons that control elements of the display, such as brightness, contrast and position (that is, you can adjust the image width and depth to fill the available screen space). Most provide an onscreen display that makes it very much easier to see what you're doing.

As we've seen, the graphics card is responsible for generating the image that appears on screen, and now is the time to tweak its settings to best effect. For instance, you might want to boost the refresh rate to take advantage of your new monitor's increased capabilities. Click Start, point to Settings, click Control Panel, and then double-click Display. Under the Settings tab, you can set the resolution (screen area) and colour depth. Click the Advanced button to access further options. Be sure to check and, if necessary, adjust the refresh rate in the Adaptor tab. Set it to the highest rate that your monitor can support at the resolution you've chosen (consult the manual for details). It's generally easier on the eyes to compromise with a lower resolution and a higher refresh rate than the other way around.

Play around with the display settings and any supplied utilities to make the most of your new monitor.

Dual monitor setup

Here's a smart thing. If you now have two monitors on your hands, it's possible to hook them both up to your computer and use them simultaneously. The main requirement is that you must be running Windows 98 or Millennium Edition, as Windows 95 does not support this feature. Assuming that your new monitor is powered by an AGP graphics card, you'll also need to install a PCI graphics cards to drive the second monitor. Of course, you may have just such a thing handy if you upgraded your graphics card at the same time as the monitor. Even if you don't have AGP, it's perfectly possible to run a dual monitor display on two PCI cards.

Simply install the secondary graphics card alongside the main card (follow the directions on p.76), plug in the secondary monitor, and switch on your PC. Windows will detect the new card/monitor combination and prompt for the drivers.

Now click Start, point to Settings, click Control Panel, and then double-click Display. In the Settings tab, you'll see a picture of two monitors side by side. Click on the monitor numbered 2 and click Yes when asked if you wish to enable it. Finally, position the secondary monitor to the left or right of the main monitor to match its position on your desk. Now you have a single Windows working space spread across two screens.

Waste not, want not. Use that old monitor to set up a dual display system.

TECHIE CORNER

Digital vs. analogue
Here's a curiosity. Computers work with digital data but traditional CRT monitors require an analogue input (i.e. a signal that varies continuously and smoothly over time: think of the sweeping hands of an analogue clock and contrast with a digital display that jumps from second to second). Thus the graphics card must convert digital image data into an analogue signal that the monitor can understand. Would it not therefore make sense to design monitors that understand digital data directly and so do away with all this translation nonsense? Yes, in a word, and the latest generation of LCD monitors does just that. Essentially, these monitors broadcast a 'cleaner' image because the signal is not subject to the losses inherent in a digital-to-analogue conversion. However, digital monitors use a new style of interface called DVI –

Digital Visual Interface – and require a graphics card equipped with a suitable output. There are several DVI interfaces on the market, but look for DVI-I (the 'I' suffix stands for 'integrated'). DVI-I graphics cards can output to either DVI monitors or, with an adapter, traditional VGA displays. For more on digital displays, look here: **http://ddwg.org**

PART  # Upgrading your keyboard

Have too many coffee spills made too many sticky keys? Did running your keyboard under the tap do more harm than good? Do key caps come flying off in all directions every time you type? Have you outgrown that cheap, flimsy, undersized device so clearly thrown in as an afterthought with your new computer system? Do you want some extra bells and whistles in the shape of shortcut keys and internet buttons? Or have sore wrists and the onset of RSI (Repetitive Strain Injury) driven you to consider an ergonomic approach?

What you need to know

Very little, in truth, but a few pointers won't go amiss.

Connector Keyboards generally have either a small 6-pin PS/2 connector or a larger 5-pin DIN connector at the end of their cables. Although you can buy adaptors to convert one to the other, it's easier by far to source a keyboard that's immediately compatible with your PC. Alternatively, if you're running Windows 98 or later, consider a USB keyboard. In this case, go for a model with a built-in USB hub since this allows you to connect a couple of low-powered devices (including perhaps a USB mouse) directly to the keyboard.

How do 26 letters and 10 digits add up to 100-plus keys?

If your new keyboard has the wrong connector for your case, get yourself an adaptor.

Those handy Windows keys are useful shortcuts.

Key count Today's keyboards come with somewhere between 101 and 107 keys as standard. Any reference in the specifications to 'Windows 95' guarantees the inclusion of three extra keys that provide quick access to the Start menu and context-sensitive menus (equivalent to a right-click with the mouse in most applications).

Ergonomics 'Ergonomic' is a marketing term, not a standard and definitely not a science. That said, ergonomic keyboards are designed to maintain a more natural hand and wrist posture, thus helping to prevent symptoms of RSI like carpal tunnel syndrome. The first time you try one, it will feel decidedly odd and distinctly *un*natural – but persevere and you'll likely be hooked. Our advice is to seek the testimony of friends and colleagues. Toying with a keyboard for 30 seconds in a shop really doesn't tell you anything.

Extras Some keyboards even have a built-in trackball which can save a lot of to-ing and fro-ing between the keyboard and the mouse. Others feature 'hot keys' that provide shortcuts to programs and frequently accessed features. Look out too for clip-on wrist rests; these can help to prevent stress even on standard, flat, non-ergonomic keyboards.

Cordless One rather tasty upgrade is a cordless keyboard. There's no great mystery – most cordless keyboards use RF (Radio Frequency) wireless technology whereby every press of a key transmits a signal to a small receiver connected to the PC. The end result is a neater desk.

Do your wrists a favour with an ergonomic design.

Under the (key) covers
There are two main manufacturing methods for keyboards. *Switch-based* devices have micro-switches under every key and click satisfyingly with every key press. *Capacitive* keyboards incorporate a single sensitive membrane beneath the keys. Every tap makes an electronic connection that sends a signal to the computer via a microprocessor. No clicks here – the keys generally have a smooth, quiet action – but capacitive keyboards tend to last longer because there are fewer bits to break. Then again, unlike switch-based keyboards, they can not usually be repaired if they go wrong. Such is life.

Installing your new keyboard

It doesn't get much easier than this. Switch off your computer, unplug the old keyboard, plug in the new one, and switch the computer back on. In most circumstances, the new device will work immediately but it may take a software program to activate any special keys and functions. As always, have any discs that came with the device to hand, along with your Windows installation CD-ROM.

Colour coding makes a simple job foolproof.

TROUBLE-SHOOTER

You're very unlikely to run into difficulties installing a keyboard. However, one possibility, albeit rare, is that you plug in a new USB keyboard, reboot, and find that you can't enter your user name or password (assuming you have password protection set up). The problem is that the USB device's driver has not yet been installed, so Windows doesn't know that the keyboard exists and thus can not recognise its commands. The workaround is to switch the PC off once more, plug in your old keyboard *while leaving the USB keyboard connected* and enter your user name and password on the old device. When Windows starts, the drivers for the USB keyboard can be installed. Next time you shut down the PC, unplug the old keyboard. You should now have no further problems. Alternatively, try clicking Cancel when the password prompt appears. This should bypass the security feature and enable the driver to be installed.

To tweak keyboard settings, click Start, point to Settings, click Control Panel, and then double-click Keyboard. The precise options available to you depend upon the make and model of the device.

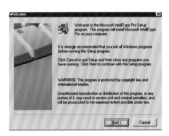

Fancier keyboards come with their own application software.

PART **Upgrading your mouse**

Cat got your mouse? Or has the poor thing just worn out? A computer mouse certainly has a finite lifespan but many people mistake a gunked-up trackball with terminal hardware failure. Have a quick glance at p.126 before consigning the poor creature to the dustbin. Otherwise, if a new mouse really is on the cards, here are the main considerations.

What you need to know

Connector Mice come with serial, PS/2 and USB connectors. In the first two cases, buy whichever is compatible with your PC – probably the same design as your current one – or be sure to get an adaptor. Some of the latest, swankiest and costliest mice are USB-only.

Buttons and wheels All mice have two clickable buttons, some have three, and many now have a central wheel nestling between the left and right buttons. You may find this awkward to use at first but it's a terrific boon for scrolling swiftly through documents and web pages. Indeed, we'd unhesitatingly recommend the wheel as sufficient reason to upgrade an old mouse.

A cordless keyboard and mouse combination means fewer cables to clutter your desk

Optical mice This style of modern mouse has an optical (light) sensor on its underbelly that detects its motion and relays this to the computer. No more de-fluffing but do use a mat because optical mice don't always work well on all surfaces.

Cordless mice If you keep snagging your mouse on desktop furniture, consider the wireless variety. Here, just like a cordless keyboard, a radio sensor plugs into the mouse port and picks up signals from the roving rodent.

Trackballs Instead of sliding a mouse around a mat, a trackball stays stationary while you move the screen cursor by manipulating a big ball, just like the arcade games of yore. Some people love them; others wouldn't give them deskroom.

Extras Some mice have four, five or six buttons onboard, some of which can be individually programmed to perform common functions. These are worth considering if you tend to use the mouse more than the keyboard.

Installing your new mouse

As with a keyboard, switch off, plug it in, switch on again and away you go. Really, it's as simple as that. Well, usually…

Optical mice run fluff-free forever.

How to upgrade your mouse: plug it in!

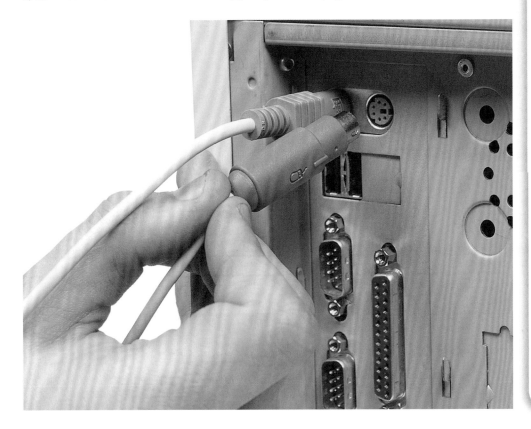

TROUBLE-SHOOTER

Windows includes a standard mouse driver that gets most devices working immediately. However, the New Hardware Found wizard might just spring into life during the first reboot, especially if you've opted for a fancy breed. If so, be ready to load the software supplied with the mouse.

Assuming that your new mouse works from the outset, install any specialist software from the supplied CD-ROM (or floppy disk) at your leisure and experiment with your new options.

To tweak mouse settings, click Start, point to Settings, click Control Panel, and then double-click Mouse. The precise options available to you depend upon the make and model of the device.

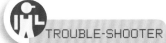

PART  Upgrading your speakers

Decent speakers can make even the crummiest sound card sound better than it deserves to, but a top-notch sound card is wasted on those tiny, tinny units usually bundled in 'free' with a computer. So, be you music lover or musician, computer games player or DVD movie fan, invest in a decent set of bins if you want to rock the house.

What you need to know

Hi-fi buffs will have little trouble with speaker specifications but the rest of us need a little help.

Subwoofers and satellites A subwoofer is a big-speaker-in-a-box that sits on the floor and boosts the bass signal. Satellites are smaller but still full-range speakers positioned left and right of the listener in order to produce a stereo effect. Such a setup is described as 2.1 (two satellites plus a subwoofer) 4.1 (four satellites plus a subwoofer) or 5.1 (guess).

Surround sound This is the effect created when a second set of speakers is positioned behind the listener, one to each side, to complement a pair of stereo speakers positioned left and right of the sound source. A separate subwoofer handles the bass tones and, in a 5.1 setup, a further satellite is positioned directly in front of the listener. A surround sound-capable sound card then pumps different elements of the audio signal to different speakers. The enveloping effect can be quite spooky.

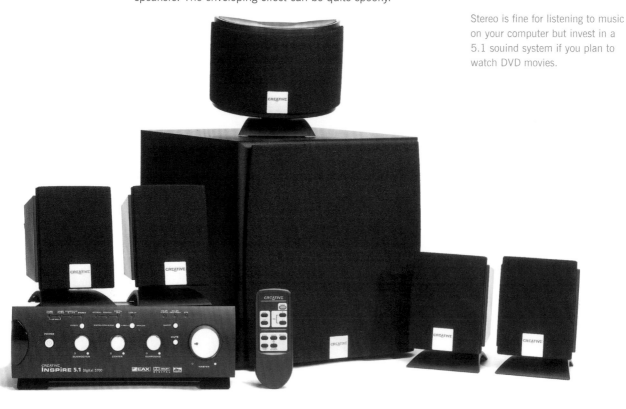

Stereo is fine for listening to music on your computer but invest in a 5.1 souind system if you plan to watch DVD movies.

High-tech speakers need to be positioned correctly and configured with software.

Digital input Most sound cards and speakers work with analogue signals but there is a digital breed as well. If your sound card happens to support digital output – look for the term S/PDIF, or Sony/Philips Digital InterFace – it's worthwhile getting digital speakers to compliment it. Otherwise, you'll be looking at a costly sound-card-plus-speakers upgrade. Is it worth it? Only your ears can answer that one.

USB Sound cards convert the digital signal from, say, an audio CD or MP3 file into an analogue signal and pipe it to the speakers. However, it's now possible to buy digital speakers that connect to the PC through the USB port, bypassing the sound card completely to pick up the digital signal at source and thereby broadcast a 'cleaner' signal. You have to be pretty committed to aural fidelity to spot the difference, and they're not the easiest things to configure, but we thought we ought to mention them.

Spaghetti This is what you get when you install a 4.1 or 5.1 speaker system. Be prepared to trip over more wiring than you thought possible and be sure to follow the setup directions carefully.

Installing your new speakers

Plug them in to the audio out channel(s) on your sound card, connect the power supply to a wall socket, and switch them on. Sounds too simple to be true? Well, yes and no. No, because hooking them up to your PC really is as straightforward as that. But yes, because you will certainly have to play around with both the speaker positions and the supplied software settings before you achieve Nirvana.

TECHIE CORNER

Going overboard
Computer audio technology, both analogue and digital, continues to evolve apace. We haven't even touched on the scientific stuff, such as signal to noise ratios and frequency responses. The bottom line is this: if you really want to use your PC as a sound system, you are truly spoilt for choice and should research the multitude of options carefully; but if you just want a decent sound quality for playing CDs and the odd game, a mid-range, mid-price multi-channel sound card and a decent set of 4.1 or 5.1 surround sound speakers will blow your socks off. To find out much, much more, go here:
http://www.dolby.com

PART  Upgrading your printer

'Free' inkjet printers are commonly included as part of the package with new computer systems. This is fine as far as it goes but it really doesn't go very far at all. Such printers tend to be bargain basement models, all but obsolete and good for only the most rudimentary, low resolution print jobs. Run off your business cards replete with jazzy logo on one of these and... well, colleagues will accept them politely but mark you down as a cheapskate amateur. And yet it's perfectly possible to buy a superb colour inkjet or monochrome laser printer for not very much money at all. So, tell the salesperson to keep the giveaway and give you a discount instead; then you can shop around for a printer that really matches your requirements.

Prints charming More on the detailed specs in a second but do take a moment to consider why you need a printer and what you want it to do for you. The first decision is to choose between an inkjet and a laser. If crisp, clear text is paramount, then a laser printer is a must. But if you'd like some colour in your life, it's got to be an inkjet.

A modern inkjet printer can produce stunning colours at a high resolution.

Some printers are geared up to print on a wide variety of media – envelopes, various paper sizes and weights, transparencies, address stickers, labels for your home-burned CDs and so forth – while others are pretty much A4 and US letter size or nothing. Some run on batteries for under-the-arm instant portability; others are specially designed to print photographs at near-professional quality; still others can print direct from a digital camera without a computer in sight. There really is a printer out there for every purpose and the prices just keep on falling.

What you need to know

It pays to research the market carefully and we'd recommend reading a few comparative group tests in computer magazines to see what's currently hot and what's not. Such is the pace of evolution that last month's super-duper photo-realistic miracle of modern engineering is invariably this month's overpriced smudger. Here's a guide to the main considerations.

Interface There are two connection choices, generally speaking: the traditional parallel port or USB. Either is fine but USB is now the default standard. Look for a network interface card – or at least the potential to add one – on a laser printer if you want to share it with colleagues in a workgroup. That said, printer sharing in a small home network is easily arranged. See Part 6.

From portable to professional, there are printers to suit every output.

Go for a USB printer if your PC supports it.

Consumables As a rule, colour inkjet printers are cheaper to buy than monochrome laser printers but more expensive to run. This is because they use one or more ink cartridges that must be replaced when they run dry. These things aren't cheap and, irritatingly, the cheapest printers often use the most expensive cartridges. Do the sums: a giveaway inkjet that costs more than its own purchase price to refill each time is not much of a bargain.

Be sure to choose a printer that uses separate black and colour ink cartridges, as there's nothing more wasteful than throwing out perfectly good colours just because the black runs out (and vice versa).

Be aware that if you're tempted to *refill* old cartridges with cheap ink – and there are plenty of companies who'll happily sell you a kit to do just that – you can save a pretty penny but you'll almost certainly invalidate the printer's warranty. The print quality is also likely to be poorer.

Insist on an inkjet printer that uses separate black and coloured ink cartridges.

TECHIE CORNER

Print technologies

The two grand *impact* printers of yesteryear were clattering, clumsy affairs. Dot-matrix models struck pins against an ink-impregnated ribbon – the greater the number of pins, the better the quality of the letters – while daisy-wheel machines hammered protruding characters on a rotating disk. Neither type could print pictures and both are now all but obsolete, certainly on the domestic desktop

(which is not to say that you won't find them bashing out despatch notes in warehouses around the world: if staff have to shout, there's an impact printer at work).

Laser printers use light to generate a charged image on a drum and heat-fuse powdery black toner on to paper. *Inkjet printers* squirt tiny globules of ink straight at the page. This used to mean that pages came out all sopping wet and soggy, but no longer. It's

all so much more refined these days, and a good deal more flexible. Even the cheapest inkjet printer suffices for homework projects and printing out web pages, and the humblest laser can produce professional quality text.

What the world is waiting for, of course, is the affordable *colour* laser printer. Such things exist and are increasing in popularity but the price premium is still pretty prohibitive.

High-quality paper is a worthwhile investment for photographic reproduction.

Laser printer

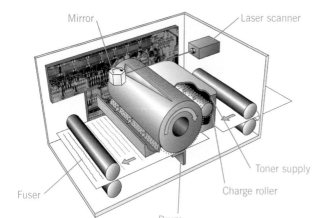

Inkjet cartridge

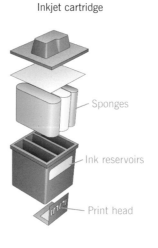

Resolution This is a rating of the level of detail in a printed image, measured in terms of dots per inch. Look for at least 600dpi or 1200dpi. Beware references to 'enhanced' or 'interpolated' resolution, as this involves software sophistry and is not a true reflection of a device's ability. Also check that a quoted resolution of 600dpi means 600 x 600 (i.e. 600 dots per inch horizontally *and* vertically). Sometimes, 600 x 300 resolutions are misleadingly described as 600dpi.

Memory Laser printers have to buffer data from the PC as they work and so incorporate RAM chips. The bare minimum is 512KB but 2 or 4MB makes for faster, more reliable performance. Many models' memory can be upgraded, which could be helpful if your work rate shoots up or you print a lot of graphics.

Speed Most manufacturers claim that their printers are capable of churning out X pages of Y-sized paper with Z% ink coverage per minute. That would be just fine if they all used the same criteria, but they don't. Sadly, it's up to you to get out the calculator and do the maths. However, do you really *care* how fast your printer is? Most domestic tasks are hardly 'mission critical' so we'd suggest concentrating more on quality than on speed.

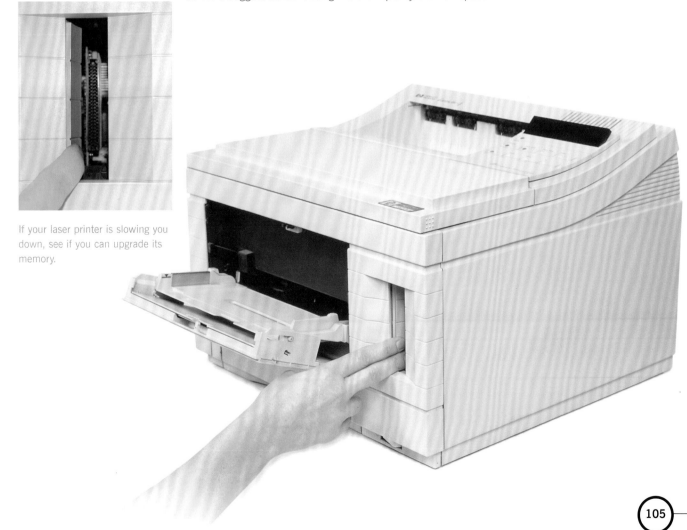

If your laser printer is slowing you down, see if you can upgrade its memory.

TECHIE CORNER

Multifunction devices
What, you may wonder, of those multifunction devices that combine a printer with a scanner with a fax machine with an answerphone in one neat, if rather bulky, unit? On the upside, such devices are cheaper to buy, use fewer cables and take up less space than separate components, and are thus particularly well suited to a small home office environment. However, do consider the implications if one particular element should happen to fail and the whole shebang gets sent away for repair. Will you suddenly find yourself faxless just because your printer's up the spout?

MFDs come in both inkjet and laser flavours, and we would strongly advise that you pay special attention to the print specifications, as this is the most central and important component. Judge an MFD primarily on the same basis that you would judge a standalone printer, and then weigh up whether the additional features justify the price. Don't forget that if your PC has a modem, you can already send and receive paperless faxes.

Media Virtually all laser printers work just fine with cheap, plain paper (so-called laser paper is just a little whiter and brighter). However, it is worth investing in specialist papers to get the best results from an inkjet. Don't feel that you necessarily have to buy same-brand, though; a little experimentation with alternative papers often pays dividends.

Duty cycle This is the manufacturer's measure of a printer's maximum workload. A monthly duty cycle of, say, 12,000 pages means just that: don't print any more than 12,000 pages in any given month if you want the device to continue performing at its peak. Clearly, this has much more relevance in an office setting than at home.

Lifespan How long is a piece of string? Keep refilling an inkjet printer when it runs dry and it should last 'forever' – or at least until you upgrade your operating system and discover that it no longer supports your now-obsolete device!

The photosensitive drum in a laser printer must be periodically replaced, usually at quite some cost. Look for a drum lifespan of somewhere between 15,000 and 30,000 pages, and be sure to factor this in when making price comparisons. Sometimes, the toner cartridge and drum are combined in a single unit.

Printers use either the parallel or a USB port.

Software You may find a whole heap of application software in the box. Inkjets typically come with a photo editing package and something along the lines of a make-your-own-greetings-cards utility. But don't be swayed by the software alone: it's not nearly as important as the hardware specifications.

Installing a new printer

All printers have a pre-installation routine that generally involves removing strategic strips of packing tape, loading the ink cartridges or toner, bolting on feeder and output trays, and perhaps running a self-test procedure. Follow the manual's instructions to the letter.

Thereafter, it's simply a case of connecting it to the PC's parallel or USB port. USB printers usually include a cable in the box but you might have to buy your own parallel cable. Look for one marked IEEE 1284, the standard which most printers require. Windows will prompt for a USB device's driver immediately but if you're installing a parallel port device, follow these steps:

Click *Start.*
Click Settings.
Click Control Panel.
Double-click Printers.

Double-click *Add Printer.*

TROUBLE-SHOOTER

If print quality isn't up to scratch, look for and run a diagnostic program. This should be included on the installation CD-ROM. Inkjet print heads benefit from periodic cleaning but this is a process controlled by software (i.e. don't take a cotton bud to an ink cartridge).
Most printers also let you perform a rudimentary self-test just by pushing a button or two on the device itself. Consult the manual.
Does Windows know that this is the default printer i.e. the one that all applications should use without asking? Return to the Printers folder (Step 1 above) and look for a big bold tick next to the appropriate icon. If it's not there, right-click the icon and select Set as Default.
Printer drivers are usually updated on a regular basis so it makes sense to visit the

manufacturer's website periodically. A new driver can often resolve bugs and glitches and may add some smart new features.
Unfortunately, printers have many moving parts and the software that turns a computer-generated digital document into a printed page is complex. In other words, lots can go wrong. The upside is that virtually all problems are easily rectified. Again, check the manual for guidance and consult the manufacturer's website.

Select *your printer make and model from the list, insert the supplied CD-ROM or floppy disk in its drive, click the Have Disk button, and tell Windows which drive to look in. When the driver has been installed, you'll be instructed to reboot the PC.*

Finally, *install any application programs supplied with the device. The manual may suggest that you run a print alignment utility before you start printing. Don't skip this step as it determines the accuracy of your prints.*

PART  **Upgrading your scanner**

A scanner takes a picture of a piece of paper and turns it into a digital image that's viewable on your computer. There, it's as simple as that. So what might you use one for?

Well, you could scan a paper document into your PC and then fax it through the modem. Or you could print out a hard copy or two and thus emulate a photocopier. You might scan recipes, magazine articles, newspaper clippings or handwritten notes and preserve them forever on your hard disk, or perhaps email them to friends as file attachments. You could scan your snapshots, remove the redeye and embarrassing ex-partners with an image editing program, and publish them on your website or in a newsletter. You might even scan every shred of paper in your possession and index and archive it all neatly on disc, so creating a truly paperless home/office. The uses for a scanner are indeed many and varied.

Like printers, 'free' scanners are often bundled with new computers to add the illusion of value but invariably they're second rate models. Plus any scanner more than a couple years old is going to be vastly outclassed by today's generation.

Flatbed is the most common design for scanners. However, there are plenty of alternatives, including truly portable pen-sized models.

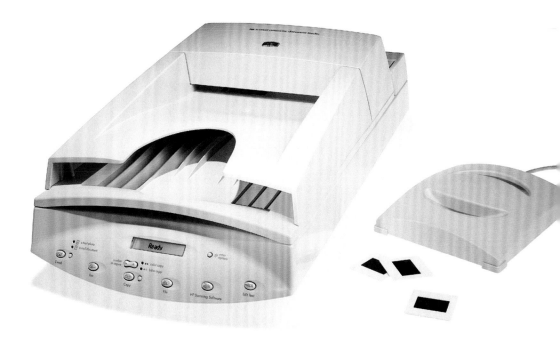

An ADF attachment saves time and effort when making multiple scans.

What you need to know

The language of scanner technology is unfamiliar to most but in fact there's nothing too complicated.

Design Scanners come in all shapes and sizes but flatbed models are by far the most popular. These look just like mini photocopiers: you lift the lid, place a document face down on the glass plate, close the lid and initiate the scan using software on your PC. Any flatbed should handle an A4 page with room to spare, and the lids are often cleverly hinged or completely removable in order that bulky objects like books also can be scanned.

Alternative designs include handheld scanners that you manually sweep across the page and sheetfeed models where you feed pages through a roller mechanism one at a time.

Interface SCSI was once common but usually meant having to install an adaptor on an internal expansion card, which was fiddly and expensive. USB is now the interface of choice but the slower parallel port also suffices.

Resolution The detail of a scanned image is measured in terms of dots per inch. More is better. Look for at least 600 x 1200dpi true, or *optical*, resolution (as opposed to *interpolated* resolution – usually a much higher figure but not a true reflection of a scanner's capability).

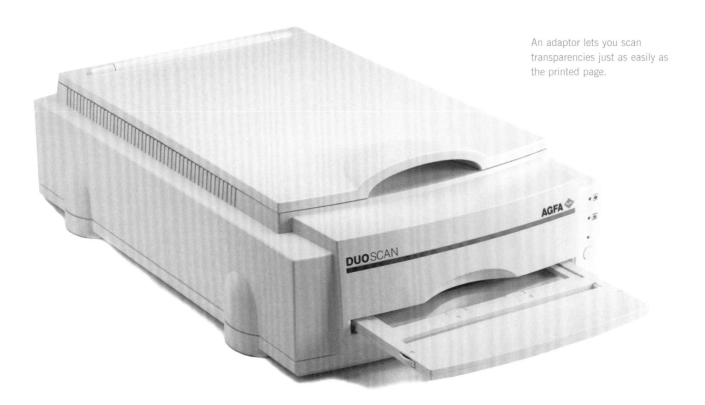

An adaptor lets you scan transparencies just as easily as the printed page.

Colour depth This describes how many colours a scanner can distinguish. Older scanners stuck at 24 bits, which equates to recognising nearly 17 million colours, but new models scan at 36 bits and are moving to 42 or even 48 bits. The greater colour depths help scanners to deal with bright and dark images as well as distinguish finer colour nuances. For scanning magazines and photos at home, a 30-bit scanner is more than adequate.

TWAIN In order for scanners to communicate with a wide range of software applications, they virtually all support a common standard called TWAIN (Technology Without An Interesting Name, according to urban legend). This means that even a word processor or spreadsheet program can import an image straight from a scanner.

ADF Strictly an optional extra, Automatic Document Feeders feed documents through a flatbed scanner one page at a time. Very useful for high volume work.

Transparency adaptor This is a bolt-on accessory with a built-in light that enables a scanner to scan photographic transparencies.

OCR If you scanned the page that you're reading right now into your computer, you might think that you could immediately cut, copy and paste the text. But you'd be wrong. A scanned page is merely an image that makes no distinction between words and pictures. OCR, or Optical Character Recognition, is the process of turning a scanned image into editable text. Essentially, software

OCR software turns a scan into editable text.

'reads' the image and determines which bits are words (and, crucially, *which* words) and which bits are design elements and pictures. OCR is almost never 100% successful but the best programs let you proof read as you go along to correct mistakes. Most scanners come with at least a 'lite' OCR package in the box.

Speed As with printers, some scanners are marginally quicker than others. The interface makes the biggest difference: SCSI scanners are quickest, parallel scanners slowest, and USB falls in the middle.

Software Look for at least a basic image manipulation program with your new toy. After all, you're going to want to tweak all those scanned images. For real ease of use, some scanners have a one-touch button that fires them into action without fussing with software. Others start working as soon as you open or close the lid. However, in most cases you'll run a TWAIN-compliant application on your PC and control the scanning process from there.

Installing your new scanner

You install a USB scanner in exactly the same way as any other USB peripheral: connect it to a free USB port on your PC and install the driver from the supplied CD-ROM or floppy disk when prompted. For a parallel model, close down the PC first, connect the scanner to the parallel port, switch on the scanner, reboot the computer, and follow the New Hardware Found wizard's directions.

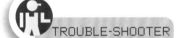

TROUBLE-SHOOTER

On the hardware front, there's nothing much to say: a scanner either works or it doesn't. Do, however, be sure to release the scan head before you make your first scan. To prevent damage in transit, it's commonplace for the scanner's moving parts (under the glass plate) to be secured with some sort of release mechanism. Check the manual for instructions.
There are usually plenty of options to play with in the application software and making a perfect scan – often a compromise between image size, resolution and colour depth – invariably takes patience and practice. Some of the best and most recent programs make scanning *almost* intuitive.

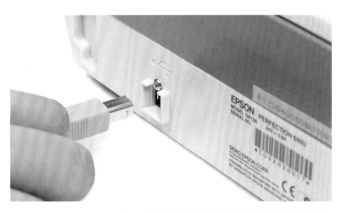

Scanners come in parallel and SCSI flavours but USB is a good compromise between speed and convenience.

PART 6 Home networking

Although you can prolong the useful lifespan of a computer almost indefinitely with well-chosen upgrades, there may come a time when you just can't resist starting afresh with a brand-new system. Or perhaps you buy a new PC for the kids, or invest in a laptop. Whatever the reasons, it is becoming increasingly common to find two or more computers in the household – at which point, when you tire of running between them transferring files on floppy disks, it makes practical sense to link them together.

PART

The basics of home networking

The benefits of networking are manifest and significant. Any computer on the network can access files stored on any other computer's hard disk; they can share a single printer regardless of which computer it happens to be connected to; and, most important of all, they can share a single connection to the internet. This means that you can have two or more computers online together without having to invest in additional phone lines.

What you need to know

Speed The most common connection standard used in home networking – or Local Area Networking (LAN) – is Ethernet. This is available in two speeds: 10Base-T, where data is transferred at a maximum rate of 10 megabits per second (see Appendix 6); and 100Base-T (also called Fast Ethernet), which runs at 10 times that. For home use, 10Base-T is ample.

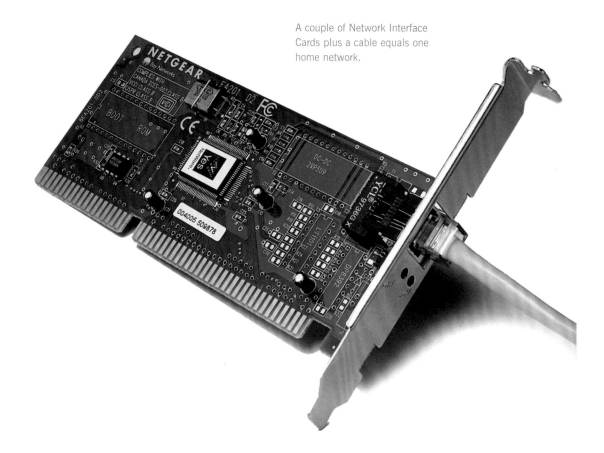

A couple of Network Interface Cards plus a cable equals one home network.

Interface Many modern PCs now come with networking capabilities built in but Ethernet can easily be added by means of a Network Interface Card (NIC). Cheaper cards support only the slower 10Base-T standard but many are sold as '10/100', which means they can run at either speed. Modern cards use the PCI interface (see p.72).

Wiring Ethernet cables come in two main flavours: coaxial and twisted pair. Some NICs have connectors for both but the most common option for home use is a twisted pair cable with RJ-45 connectors on either end. An RJ-45 connector looks like a larger version of the RJ-11 connector on your modem cable (see p.158). Always buy 'Category 5' cables because they support both types of Ethernet speed and can be reused if you ever upgrade your network from 10Base-T to 100Base-T.

Hubs and switches A hub is a box that sits between networked computers to facilitate the free flow of data. Hubs are generally pretty dumb and play no active part in managing data flow, but some incorporate switches that 'intelligently' control the traffic. A switch can avoid networking bottle-necks but it's certainly not essential for a small home network.

Topology Local Area Networks can be set up in many ways. By far the simplest is a peer-to-peer arrangement, in which each PC is an equal partner on the network. The alternative is a client-server model where one computer – the server – controls all the action. This is definitely overkill and over-complicated for home use.

Software As we shall see, it is easy to set up home networking without using any extra software if your PC runs Windows Millennium Edition (Me). Windows 98 Second Edition introduced Internet Connection Sharing, which was a big step forward from Windows 95's limited networking capabilities, but the Home Networking Wizard in Me is a pretty compelling reason to upgrade from 98 if you're serious about networking. The latest version of Windows, XP, makes networking a complete cakewalk. However, its system requirements are too high for many older systems, so we'll assume here that you have Me on board.

An RJ-45 Ethernet cable.

A peer-to-peer network is perfect for hooking together two PCs but a hub adds expansion possibilities.

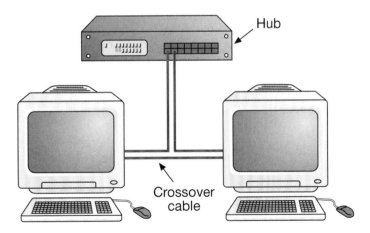

Hub

Crossover cable

PART ⑥ A simple crossover cable network

You can connect any two PCs quickly and easily with a couple of Network Interface Cards and a single cable. This is what we'll look at first.

① **Keep** *things simple by buying a pair of identical 10Base-T or 100Base-T cards with RJ-45 ports. You'll also need a Category 5 crossover cable. This is not a standard Ethernet cable but rather one in which the wiring has been specially manipulated to enable the two-way flow of data without the need for a hub. Ask for help if you're in any doubt.*

② **Install** *one Network Interface Card in the first computer. The method is identical to adding any PCI expansion card (see, for example, the step-by-step USB card upgrade on p.87). Follow the card manufacturer's instructions and install the driver software when prompted.*

③ **Data** *passes through a network according to a strict set of rules, or protocol, and the software that comes with your NIC should ensure that all necessary components are installed. Click Start, Settings, Control Panel and double-click the Network icon. In the Configuration tab, you should see entries for at least one of these protocols: NetBEUI, IPX/SPX or TCP/IP.*

④ *Also ensure that Client for Microsoft Networks is the selected entry from the Primary Network Logon drop-down list. If it is not there, click the Add button, highlight Client in the next window, click Add, select Client for Microsoft Networks, and click Add once again. Have your Windows installation CD to hand in case you are prompted for it.*

⑤ *Still in the Configuration area of the Network dialogue box, click the File and Print Sharing button and place a tick in both boxes. This ensures that you will be able to access files and print documents across the network.*

⑥ *Finally, look in the Identification tab and give your computer a meaningful name and, optionally, description. Type MSHOME in the Workgroup field. Close the Network dialogue and restart when prompted. Now install the second NIC in the second PC, repeat each of these steps, and connect the two computers by plugging the crossover cable into the NICs.*

Home Networking Wizard

To get your fledgling network up and running, you need to tell each computer a little about how it is expected to behave. In Windows Millennium Edition, double-click the My Network Places icon on the Desktop, run the Home Networking Wizard and follow the prompts. It's pretty much plain sailing but here are the important points to note:

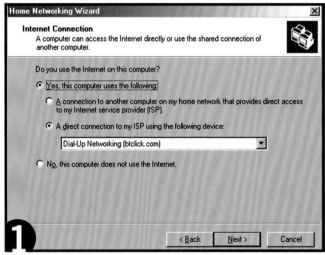

Start *with the PC that you usually use for internet access (i.e. the one with a modem connected to the telephone line). When the Internet Connection dialogue box appears, check the 'direct connection to my ISP' option. Later, when you run the wizard on the second PC, be sure to check the 'connection to another computer on my home network' option. This sets up internet connection sharing.*

The *wizard will ask you for the name of your workgroup and recommend that you accept the default suggestion of MSHOME. This is just fine: the important point is that all computers on a network must use the same workgroup name. You can also rename your computer at this point if you wish.*

Now *you will be asked if you want to share folders and printers. Accept the recommendation to share the My Documents folder and place a tick against any printers currently connected. You can also add password protection at this point but we'd suggest leaving this until later.*

Finally, *the wizard will ask if you wish to make a Home Networking Setup disk. This makes it easier to configure all other computers in your network but it's hardly worthwhile when you have only the two to worry about. Instead, simply run the wizard on the second PC now. Restart both computers when prompted.*

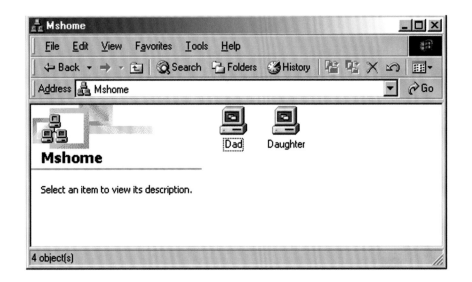

Networked computers in the same workgroup can share files and an internet connection.

Sharing

Double-click the My Network Places (or Network Neighborhood) icon again, double-click Entire Network, and then double-click MSHOME (or whatever name you gave to your workgroup). You should now be able to 'see' the other networked computer. Click its icon and have a look in its My Documents folder. Try dragging and dropping files from one PC to the other. That's the wonder of networking!

It's easy to extend or restrict file and folder sharing in a network. For instance, you might wish to provide unrestricted access to one computer's entire hard disk. Double-click My Computer, right-click the hard disk icon (C: drive), select Sharing, and then check the Shared As option. Every file and folder on this disk can now be seen, copied, modified and – importantly – deleted by someone using the other networked PC. Hence the importance of password protection: with drive and folder sharing, you have the opportunity to control the limits of network access. Read-Only access, for instance, means that someone who knows your password can use your files but not delete or modify them.

CD, DVD and Zip drives can be shared in exactly the same way as a hard disk.

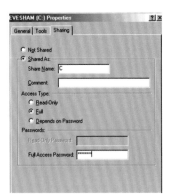

Use passwords to protect your files.

TROUBLE-SHOOTER

• Although a simple peer-to-peer home network should 'just work', there will be times when one computer doesn't 'see' the other(s). In our experience, the best solution is to restart one, both or all the PCs to reconnect the network. You can also run the Home Networking Wizard at any time to check each computer's settings. Do remember that each computer on the network must have a unique name and that they must all use the same workgroup.

• If you have problems with shared internet access, try running the Internet Connection Wizard (click Start, Programs, Accessories and Communications) on the networked PC that doesn't connect directly to the internet. Select 'I want to connect through a local area network' and then tick the 'Automatic discovery of proxy server' option.

• Windows 98 users don't have the advantage of the Home Networking Wizard but it's still possible to get your computers connected. Look here for help from Microsoft:

http://www.microsoft.com/ windows98/usingwindows/ work/articles/906network/ homeoverview.asp

• Beyond the basics networking is a big, sometimes complex, subject. Here are some excellent web links for further information and advice:

http://www.homepcnetwork.com http://www.practically networked.com http://www.howstuffworks.com/ home-network.htm http://www.microsoft.com/ homenet

PART ⑥ Taking it further

The advantages of a crossover cable connection as described above are that it's simple to set up and requires little in the way of hardware. However, there is one serious limitation: there is no way to hook up any further PCs. In other words, your network has no scope for expansion. So...

Hub networking made simple with a kit.

Kitting up

The good news is that you set up a hub-based network in just the same way as a crossover connection. The only real difference is that you use standard (i.e. non-crossover) Ethernet cables and connect each PC to the hub rather than directly to each other. It's possible to buy complete network-in-a-box kits that include a couple of NICs, a hub and all the cables you need. Some also come with software that gets everything up and running first time more easily than the Home Networking Wizard. Be sure to check the speed rating on the hub and cards – 10Base-T or 100Base-T – and note the number of available ports on the hub (you need one for every PC on the network).

Going wireless

As if you didn't have enough computer wiring to trip over already, home networking generally requires you to run cables from room to room in order to connect your computers. However, if you're feeling flush, consider the wireless alternative. Today's most prolific technology is known as 802.11b, or Wi-Fi: a wireless transmission standard that operates at a maximum speed of up to 11 megabits per second (i.e. faster than a basic wired Ethernet network). This a particularly attractive option for laptop owners since you can tap into the full resources of your network at will without fussing with cables: all you need is a removable PC card in the laptop and a wireless access point connected to the network hub. The range for wireless networking varies but you can expect to maintain a fast, unbroken connection over a distance of at least 100 metres.

Who needs cables? Take your laptop to the garden.

PART

PC maintenance

Computer hardware is a curious mix of solid-state components with no moving parts to break or seize and precision-engineered, finely-tuned devices that require regular maintenance and cleaning to work at their best. Things can and do go wrong so here we consider some sensible preventative measures to stop potential problems in their tracks, some basic trouble-shooting techniques, and a maintenance regime designed to keep your PC running smoothly.

PART 7

Windows utilities

As you might expect, Windows (95/98/Me/XP) comes equipped with an array of useful tools designed to optimise its own performance. While many people swear by the likes of Norton SystemWorks or McAfee Office, others never spend a penny on third-party utility software. We'll consider commercial alternatives shortly but for now let's look at what Windows itself has to offer.

Defragmenting your hard disk improves performance.

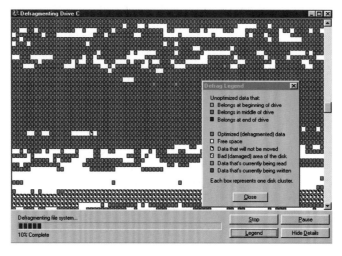

Disk Defragmenter

The data on your hard disk is stored in lots of small packets. Although this is an efficient use of space, one side effect is that individual files can get split apart and stored piecemeal all over the disk. This process is known as fragmentation and it only gets worse with time. Every time you open a fragmented file, Windows has to track down all the different bits and pieces and stick them back together again – a time-consuming and wasteful business. However, with a utility called Disk Defragmenter, you can restore all files to their former glory and buck up system performance at a stroke.

Close down all programs before running Disk Defragmenter.

It's important to close down all system activity before you begin as any attempt by a program to write data to the hard disk causes Disk Defragmenter to start from scratch. Close all running programs like your word processor, browser or email program in the usual way, and disconnect from the internet. You should end up with a clear Desktop and no buttons on the Taskbar. Then look in the System Tray – the part of the Taskbar next to the clock – for icons that show which programs are running in the background. Right-click each icon in turn and select Exit or Close. You should be left with just the clock and speaker icons.

Finally, press the Ctrl, Alt and Delete keys simultaneously. This reveals any other open, but hidden, applications. Highlight each item in turn – *with the exception of Explorer and Systray* – and select Shut Down.

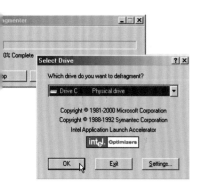

Tell the program which disk to work on.

Now click Start, Programs, Accessories and System Tools. Here you will find Disk Defragmenter. Start the program and select the drive you wish to repair (usually C: drive).

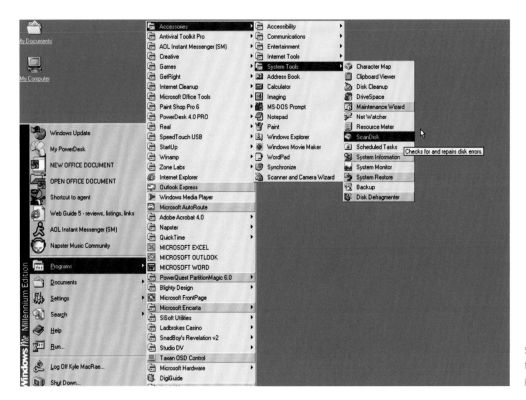

System Tools isn't the easiest folder to find but it hosts several good utilities.

ScanDisk

Whenever your PC crashes or closes down unexpectedly, you may notice that it runs through an error checking process next time you start it up. This is ScanDisk looking for, and hopefully fixing, file problems on the hard disk. However, you can also run ScanDisk on demand. Here's how.

Click Start, Programs, Accessories, System Tools and ScanDisk. There are two options here: a Standard test, which is reasonably quick and checks all your files and folders for errors; and a Thorough test, which takes much longer but also examines the physical integrity of your hard disk. If you're having problems with your PC – perhaps a document won't open – the Standard test is usually enough, but we'd recommend a Thorough scan once in a while as part of a periodic system maintenance regime.

Check the box marked 'Automatically fix errors' to speed things up. You can set the parameters of what ScanDisk will and will not do in the Advanced dialogue box but the default options are just fine. As with Disk Defragmenter, leave ScanDisk to work in peace.

If it finds any lost clusters (parts of files), it saves them with the extension .CHK in the root directory (the topmost folder in Windows). These may safely be deleted. If, however, ScanDisk reports any 'bad sectors', back-up your files immediately. Although Windows will not now write any new data to these unusable areas of the hard disk, it may be a sign of impending disk failure.

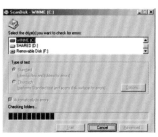

Let ScanDisk automatically fix any problems it finds.

Disk Cleanup

Programs take up a lot of space but so can individual files, particularly web pages saved to the hard disk by your web browser. Disk Cleanup can automatically remove a good deal of this debris.

As with Disk Defragmenter and ScanDisk, Disk Cleanup is found in the System Tools menu. The program offers several options: simply check each box in turn for an explanation of what it does. Do be cautious about emptying the Recycle Bin, especially if you've just deleted a bunch of files. Sure as eggs is eggs you'll wish you hadn't permanently consigned that complete record of your household finances to oblivion three seconds after you push the button.

The Temporary Internet Files section may be quite large. This is your browser's cache – an area of your hard disk set aside for keeping copies of the web pages you visit. If you delete its contents, your browser will have to reload each page from scratch next time you revisit a favourite site instead of plucking some or all of its elements from the cache. This may slow down your surfing a little but the cache soon fills up again and the effects are short-lived. Besides, many web pages are updated frequently so having an old copy on your computer isn't really much of an advantage.

Disk Cleanup explains what it's going to do before it starts.

Don't let rubbish clog up your hard disk.

Maintenance Wizard

The problem with ScanDisk, Disk Defragmenter and Disk Cleanup is, of course, that you'll never remember to use them. That's why Windows includes Maintenance Wizard, a utility that lets you set up an automatic schedule for running one, two or all three programs at regular intervals. Once again, find it by clicking Start, Programs, Accessories and System Tools, and then run Maintenance Wizard in custom mode. Note that it's best to schedule these tasks to run at a time when you're not using your computer, like the middle of the night. You also have to ensure that no running programs will interfere with Disk Defragmenter (see above), so close down anything that's not absolutely essential and deactivate any screensaver before you bed down. Oh, and don't forget to leave your computer switched on and running.

If you're prone to forgetfulness, what you want is a Wizard.

Drive Converter

If you're still obstinately running Windows 95 and refuse to upgrade, far be it for us to question your choice. However, you might at least care to consider a simple way of improving the way in which Windows manages your disk space.

In Windows 95, the minimum unit of file storage is 32 kilobytes. This means that a saved 10K file, for example, effectively wastes 22K of disk space. However, there are two options to improve this state of affairs. First, if your hard disk is smaller than 500MB, Windows automatically switches to a more efficient 4K cluster size. (Even if your disk is bigger than 500Mb, you could partition it into smaller segments and thus fool Windows into treating each partition as a separate disk.)

Alternatively, convert your filing system to the vastly more efficient FAT32 model with Drive Converter, a Windows utility located in the System Tools menu. Unfortunately, the very first release of Windows 95 does not include Drive Converter. Click Start, Settings, Control Panel, System and look in the General tab of System Properties. If your version of Windows 95 ends with the letter *a*, you're out of luck.

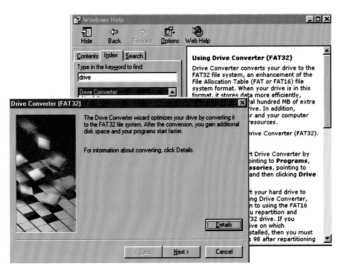

Changing to the FAT32 file system improves disk management in Windows 95.

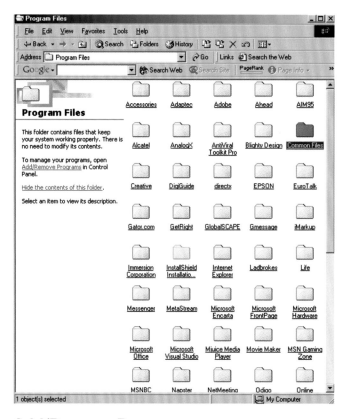

How many of your programs do you actually use?

Add/Remove Programs

Ah, if only life was simple and you could install and delete software at will and with ease. Well, sometimes you can, but only sometimes. The trouble is that there's no single, catch-all, foolproof method for ridding a system of unwanted applications. Some come with their own uninstall utilities while others rely on Windows to do the work. Still others display a thoroughly leech-like determination to never be deleted.

One of the requirements for a product to carry the 'Designed for Windows 95' logo on the box is compliance with Microsoft's InstallShield standard. A 'true' Windows program should install smoothly and do away with itself just as easily. However, in practice, bits and pieces of programs are often left behind, notably empty folders and scattered cryptic files. Most worrying are orphaned entries in the Windows Registry, a record of all that makes your system tick. Conflicts and confusion in here can be serious. Windows XP controls rogue programs far more effectively than its predecessors, to the extent that it objects in the strongest possible terms if you try to install something that hasn't been tested and automatically backs up and restores any critical system files that are altered during installation or use.

But why bother getting shot of old software? Why not just let it be? Three reasons:

1 Old programs take up disk space. Sooner or later, you're liable to need it, so it's better to manage this as you go along

2 You might not realise it but many programs run continuously in the background even if you never actually use them to do anything useful. This eats into available RAM and has a detrimental effect on performance

3 Every additional program on your system increases the risk of a conflict with another, more useful program. As a rule, tidy systems run more smoothly, and you may find that simply uninstalling some half-forgotten software miraculously cures no end of unexplained ills.

Deletion Completion

So, click Start and Programs and see just what you've got onboard. Point at any superfluous programs and see if an Uninstall option appears. If so, select it and follow the step-by-step instructions. At the end of the process, you may be warned that some elements of the program must be manually removed. Make a note of any details supplied. The leftovers are usually a top-level folder in the Program Files menu and perhaps one or two sub-folders within. Now click My Computer, select your hard disk, click Program Files and find the folder(s) that you jotted down. These may now be dragged straight to the Recycle Bin. Incidentally, Windows Millennium Edition has the touching habit of refusing you access to Program Files on pain of the sky falling in. Just override it.

Where a program doesn't come with its own uninstaller, click Start, Settings, Control Panel and Add/Remove programs. This brings up a list of programs that Windows can automatically delete. Just highlight the program and click Add/Remove.

Some programs thoughtfully have their own uninstall option.

Add/Remove Programs clear out the clutter. Unfortunately, it doesn't always work perfectly.

PC MAINTENANCE

Third party utilities

The shelves of your local computer superstore are stacked with commercial utility software that promises to make amends for the failings of Windows and keep your PC running in tip-top condition for ever and a day. Bold claims indeed, and not wholly without merit. With all such packages, there is a significant overlap with Windows' own utilities and, in the case of the major suites, often some internal features overlap as well. But the real point of these programs is threefold:

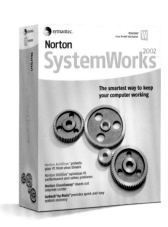

1 Routine maintenance tasks like defragmenting a hard disk and trouble-shooting hardware conflicts are faster, more efficient and above all easier to manage than with Windows alone.

2 You get value-added extra features into the bargain (see below).

3 Peace of mind. You don't have to be paranoid to believe that sooner or later your computer will self-destruct and take with it all your precious data, or that hackers will break into your system, steal your credit card number and make merry with your money. There's a good deal more hype than substance in these scare stories but the bottom line is that people feel safer with added security measures in place.

The kitchen sink approach The big players in the utility software stakes are Norton (a division of Symantec), McAfee (a division of Network Associates) and Ontrack. All three produce fully-fledged utility suites that bundle all their many programs together and offer the best overall value for money. All three also offer a range of standalone products that specialise in particular areas and offer enhanced tools. We are not inclined to recommend any one product over any other, or indeed to say that you absolutely *need* any utility software at all. But here's a quick rundown on the central features to look out for when shopping around. Note that all utilities slow your system down to some extent but that's the payoff for added stability.

Trouble-shooting It's usual to find a 'one-click-solves-all-woes' button in utility suites these days, and certainly you can save a great deal of time and effort by letting smart software seek out and resolve your system conflicts. Hardware and software issues alike can be treated, including deep-rooted Windows problems.

Crash protection A utility that stops an impending crash in its tracks and gives you the chance to save your work is worth its weight in gold. Unfortunately, results tend to be variable.

Program uninstaller Dedicated program uninstallers that do a thorough job of deleting old software.

Zip utility What better way to save disk space and tidy up than by compressing multiple files into one much smaller file, called an 'archive'? Zips are commonly used on the internet to reduce the duration of file transfers. Download the evaluation version of WinZip before splashing out elsewhere: **www.winzip.com.**

Disk imaging This is the process of copying, or 'cloning', an entire hard disk in one move, up to and including the operating system, in order to load it on another computer or to recover the current system in the event of a disaster.

Firewall A program that stops hackers from gaining access to your computer.

Web services Look for a feature that scans your system to see what software you have installed and automatically finds any available upgrades, patches and bug fixes.

Encryption Want to keep your email or documents on your hard disk files secret? Then you'll be wanting a file encryption tool.

File recovery Deleted an important document by mistake? File recovery utilities can (sometimes) help.

And then, of course, there's anti-virus software. But that, we strongly suggest, is not an optional extra. Read on…

See what's going on under the hood.

Programs keep crashing? Utility software can help save your work.

Many utilities do much the same as Windows, but usually rather better.

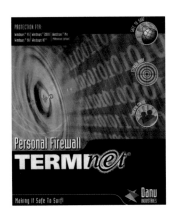

A full utility suite may have 20 or 30 separate programs.

PART

Viruses – a special case

However you cut it, computer viruses are a fact of life. At best, they're a hassle; at worst, downright destructive. You have to be something of a moron to release one 'in the wild', so to speak, but there's no shortage of them in the world. And so all we can do is accept that viruses are with us in abundance and take adequate precautions.

Update your anti-virus software frequently.

Protect and survive

Viruses are basically programs like any other. They typically have two parts: a means of getting into your system, and a reason for doing so. Once inside, a successful virus might scramble your data, sit quietly in the background doing nothing at all until triggered by a key date, or instantly email copies of itself to everyone in your address book. Some viruses are created by geeks for the supposed kudos of being clever with code; others are written by malicious saboteurs bent on wreaking havoc across company networks or the internet itself. In all cases, your first and necessary line of defence is to install an anti-virus program. This attempts to identify inbound nasties in one or both of two ways: by spotting and isolating known viruses (highly effective but not much use against brand new bugs that aren't yet in its database); and by looking for suspiciously virus-like behaviour (a good safety net, although far from foolproof).

If you suspect you've been infected, scan your system without delay.

Moreover, because new viruses appear all the time, you must update your anti-virus program regularly. If it has an auto-update feature, all to the good: allow it to call home for updates whenever you're online. Otherwise, make it a point of principle to manually update it *at least* once a month, and preferably once a week. Some developers now release daily updates. Remember – an out of data anti-virus program is next to worthless, so don't assume that you're safe just because your new computer came with an anti-virus program pre-installed.

Get wise to hoaxes

Don't be fooled by silly hoaxes – check them out on the web.

Equally important is making sure that you don't contribute to the spread of these pests yourself. Never pass on a virus warning without first checking whether or not it's a hoax. If a rampant email virus can bring a network to a standstill, a flurry of hoax warnings is almost as damaging. So, if you get a virus warning in your email inbox, pause and consider before forwarding it to anybody else. Does it exhort you in the strongest possible terms to tell everybody you know 'WITHOUT DELAY!!!!'? Does it proclaim that unspeakable things will happen to your hard disk if you get infected? Does it read like the work of an idiot trying to get a rise out of the world? Then it's almost certainly a hoax. Check it out at Vmyths.com (**http://vmyths.com**) before you pass it on.

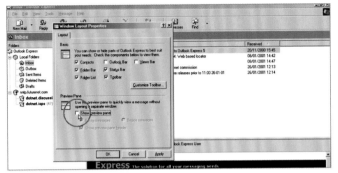

Switch off the Preview Pane option in your email program for better security.

Scan your computer for viruses on the web with McAfee.

Periodically check for Windows updates and install any security patches.

Sensible steps

Aside from installing and updating anti-virus software, there are various things you can do to minimise the risk of infection.

Switch on your anti-virus program's background scanning features to ensure that all files are checked at the point of being opened.

Check for security updates and patches for your email program. If you use Microsoft's Outlook or Outlook Express, go here: **http://windowsupdate.microsoft.com**

Don't download files from strangers on the internet, and delete, without opening, any unasked for email attachments. Don't even sneak a peek at mystery messages in your email program's Preview Pane, as this alone can be enough to do the damage. For maximum security, switch off the Preview Pane option altogether. In Outlook Express, click Layout in the View menu and uncheck the Preview Pane option.

Be wary of Word documents (files with the extension .DOC) and Excel spreadsheets (extension .XLS), as these could harbour macro viruses.

Never open an executable file type unless and until you've scanned it for viruses *and* been personally assured by the sender that it's safe. Extensions to look out for include: .EXE, .VBS and .JS.

Don't beg, steal or borrow dodgy software.

Beware of files that try to hide their true extension e.g. BritneySpearsNaked.jpg.vbs. Many a mug would assume that this is a harmless image file but the .VBS extension gives the game away: it's a script virus.

If you don't already have an anti-virus program up and running, give your system a quick health check online with McAfee Clinic: **http://www.mcafee.com**

TECHIE CORNER

Virus types
The computer virus comes in many different guises and it helps to know a little about how they operate. That said, the bottom line is that they're all a menace and to be avoided at all costs.

Worm A program that creates copies of itself, each of which creates more copies, and so on. Think of cell division. Worms spread through email, usually without your knowledge and always without your permission.

Trojan A virus that masquerades as something desirable – perhaps a useful utility – but is really the carrier for a malicious payload.

Macro A program hidden within a word processor document or spreadsheet, usually with a destructive capacity.

Script virus Like a macro virus but written in a dynamic computing language like JavaScript.

For a full run-down, check Symantec's database here: **http://securityresponse. symantec.com/avcenter/ vinfodb.html**

Taking precautions

A little foresight and rudimentary background knowledge about the various things that can do a computer system harm goes a long way towards averting serious problems. We covered static electricity at the very outset and we'll take the liberty of assuming that you already know that water and electricity don't mix (i.e. don't play with your PC in the bath). Here are some other essentials.

A lightning strike could fry your computer – so better get protected!

Magnetism

If it wasn't for the magic of magnetism, your PC's hard disk couldn't permanently store data. Nor could floppy or Zip disks transfer files from here to there and back again. But while magnetism is undoubtedly a force for good, it can also do inordinate damage to your data when allowed to interfere with the strictly controlled conditions present in your computer system. It pays, therefore, to be aware that magnets *in any form* and data stored on magnetic media (as opposed to optical media like CD-ROMs and DVD discs) do not come into contact with one another.

For instance, never stick a magnetic paper clip holder on your PC case lest it interfere with the workings of the hard disk. Keep floppies well away from magnetic sources like printers, fridges, cars, mobile phones, hi-fi speakers – and, of course, plain

Degaussing your monitor clears up odd screen effects caused by stray magnetism.

magnets. It's also unwise to stack them on top of the PC case. As we've mentioned before, a magnetic screwdriver may be perfect for retrieving lost screws but it shouldn't be allowed anywhere near the inside of a computer.

Speakers designed for use with a computer are usually shielded in order to prevent (most of) the magnetic field from interfering with the system. But if you site them too close to a CRT monitor, they can affect the flow of electrons that makes up the display image. The result is often patches of light, dark or odd colours on the screen, and this can cause permanent damage if left unchecked. It's also prudent to keep your monitor some distance away from the main PC case to prevent any possible interference between its own magnets and the hard disk.

However, a short-term problem is easily resolved by 'degaussing' the monitor to realign the magnetic fields. There may be a degauss button on the monitor itself or you may find an option in any utility software that came with the monitor. Check the manual for details.

Power surges

You may well have a good idea of just how regular, or smooth, your electricity supply is. Then again, you may have no idea. Peaks and dips are sometimes made evident by an unexpected brightening or dimming of the lights, but a *serious* peak, or spike, can do a computer serious damage.

Now, all reputable PC manufacturers build some form of surge protection into the power supply controlling the current that flows into the system but it's unwise to rely on this alone. If you consider that you're at risk from sudden voltage spikes, or if you simply want an added layer of protection, consider a heavy-duty surge protector. This is a circuit breaker sited between your computer and the electricity supply that stops any spike in its tracks.

There are several different designs but the most effective deploy a metal-oxide varistor (MOV) that routes the surge straight to earth and thus out of harm's way. Unfortunately, these can be worn down over time and a single large surge may kill an MOV outright. This is fine – after all, it's the job of a surge protector to take the bullet for your computer – but, rather bizarrely, some units don't actually tell you when the MOV is dead. To avoid an unwarranted sense of security, be certain to buy a surge protector with a warning light that clearly displays whether or not it's working!

The most dramatic power surge of all is, of course, a lightning strike, and here again it pays to be protected. The first thing to do at the first sign of a storm is to switch off and unplug the computer from the wall. Don't forget the cable linking the modem to the telephone socket, as lightning will be only too happy to follow a path through the telephone wiring to your PC's motherboard, leaving you with a fried system, a daunting repair bill, and quite possibly a small electrical fire. Please don't follow the example of one hapless consumer who waited patiently for Windows to shut down correctly while the wrath of the gods unfurled in the skies above.

A UPS unit keeps you going – for a while – when the power fails.

Power cuts

Spikes aren't the only power problem to afflict the computer user. Who hasn't experienced a sudden power cut and lost a minute, an hour or a day's work in a flash? Such incidents generally prove a great crash course in the importance of saving your work regularly as you go along but it's a lesson we could all do without. The answer is to invest in an uninterruptible power supply (UPS) of some sort. A UPS is essentially a battery unit that draws its charge from the mains supply and takes over power supply duties the instant a power outage occurs. Different models offer different levels of protection – some may provide only a few minutes power while others can keep a PC running for an hour or two (plenty of time to leap out of bed in the middle of the night, drive to the office and salvage that vital company backup job) – but the principle is simply to give you sufficient time to save your work and close down the computer in an orderly manner.

So, next time you're doing something *really* important with your PC, consider the implications if the power was suddenly to fail and use that as the basis on which to decide whether or not a UPS is warranted. Then again, if you never do anything that could be remotely construed as important or mission critical with your computer, save your money. Incidentally, the better UPS units have surge protection features too, so what better way to kill – or rather save – two birds with one stone?

On or off?

Most of us probably switch off our PC when we're finished with it and fire it up afresh the next time we need it. But have you considered that all this off- and on-ing might actually stress its components? Opinion is sharply divided on this matter. Some people swear by leaving a computer on around the clock, day after day, month after month, and it's true that modern hardware is built to run continuously at a carefully regulated temperature. Certainly, the chances of a drive failing are much higher when spinning up or down, and how would you like being brought up to operating temperature in just a few seconds if you'd been left in a bitterly cold room all weekend? But to many it just seems counter-intuitive and wasteful to leave a machine running when it's not in use. It's really a personal judgment call more than a case of right or wrong, but do bear the following points in mind:

Don't switch your computer off and on more than absolutely necessary. Note that *warm* booting your PC (hitting the reset switch or using the Ctrl-Alt-Delete keyboard combination to restart the system) doesn't count: it's cold booting (using the main power switch) that allegedly does the damage.

Don't leave your PC running unless you have a good surge protection system in place.

Do use your PC's power saving features to reduce energy drain. In particular, set the monitor to switch off after a few minutes inactivity and the hard disk to go into 'sleep' mode after perhaps an hour's idleness.

Do ensure that any computer connected to a network has adequate protection against hackers. You don't want your documents to disappear while you doze.

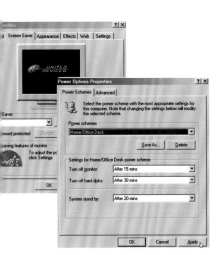

If your PC has power-saving features, it makes sense to use them.

Switching off your PC feels like the right thing to do but it's not strictly necessary.

TECHIE CORNER

Don't let the techies get you down
We're the first to say that calling a technical support telephone service should be a last resort, not your first port of call (not least because you typically pay through the nose and by the minute for such services). But if you have to seek professional help, be prepared to give a full and clear description of the apparent problem and make sure that you're by your PC. Technical support lines are (on the whole) manned by sympathetic and helpful professionals, but they are not (on the whole) mind-readers: help them to understand what's gone wrong and they'll be better placed to help you.

And before you call, remember this (probably apocryphal) story. One hapless individual rang technical support to complain that the document she had been working on had just disappeared on her screen. The engineer ran through the usual gamut of possible problems and, baffled, finally asked her to check the cables around the back of her computer – just in case. She retorted that it was too dark to see and, no, she couldn't switch on the light because of the power failure. The techie's sage advice? Return the system to the shop and ask for a full refund on account of being far too stupid to own a computer.

135

PART 7 Cleaning your PC

Keeping your computer clean won't make it run faster or crash less frequently, but it will:

Minimise the risk of passing germs and bugs from one user to another

Reduce the chance of over-heating and short-circuits

Make it look better

Just two words of warning. Don't go slopping around with a big wet sponge: your computer may come up smelling of roses but it most definitely won't work. And, of course, if you leave it plugged in while you clean, you may not live long enough to see the results. So unplug everything now, give yourself space and time enough to work in comfort, roll up your sleeves – and let's begin.

Surface cleaning

It's safe to clean pretty much every surface area with a dilute mixture of water and detergent, including the PC case, the monitor housing and all your peripherals. However, use only a *barely damp* cloth, avoid any exposed areas like printer parts and drive bays, and don't touch glass areas like the monitor screen or

A specialist cleaning fluid makes light work of spring cleaning.

A fluffy fan can lead to overheating so always make sure that it's clean.

scanner plate. If you come across a circuit board, steer *well* clear. For better results, at a price, invest in a can of computer cleansing fluid, foam or mousse. This can cut through the grease and grime in a flash.

Pay particular attention to the protective grill that encases the main ventilation fan (around the back of the PC case), as a clogged grill reduces the flow of air to the fan and increases the risk of over-heating. Carefully but thoroughly tease out the fluff. Tweezers or a toothbrush (preferably an old one, or at least not your own) can help here.

Monitor

Why some people feel compelled to touch monitor screens with sticky fingers, we know not – but they do, and they invariably leave greasy fingerprint trails behind as evidence. Quite why others contrive to sneeze all over their screens is another mystery, but we won't dwell on what *they* leave behind. Smoke, too, is drawn to monitors through static electricity and can soon come to coat the screen with a fine, filthy film.

To rid yourself of such stuff, the light dusting with a dry cloth recommended in the monitor's manual is unlikely to suffice. However, the screen is delicate indeed and any ammonia-based cleanser will completely destroy its protective coating. So, we strongly suggest that you purchase a specialist screen cleaner, preferably one with anti-static properties that helps reduce the further build up of muck. Be sure to use a lint-free cloth.

Be very, very careful when cleaning your screen! Only use a dry cloth or materials designed specifically for the job.

Clean out the innards of your mouse for jitter-free operation.

A blast of compressed air is better than a shake.

Keyboard and mouse

Keyboards are great hoarders of crumbs, hair, dust, flaky skin, dandruff and spillages of all descriptions. You can usually shake some of this detritus clear by simply turning it upside down but there's a risk that bits will accumulate under the key caps. In time, this can affect the smooth operation of the keyboard. A better bet is to blow the dirt away with a can of compressed air, sometimes called an air duster. These typically come with nozzle attachments that let you get right between the keys and squirt at the heart of the trouble.

One remarkably common computer complaint is that the onscreen cursor starts jerking around when once it ran smoothly. This is a sure sign of a gummed-up mouse. Look on its underside for a retaining ring. Unscrew this and remove the ball. Now you should see three little rollers, probably entwined with fibres and fluff. Clean these carefully with a toothbrush and blow away any loose particles. Now give the ball a quick wipe and reassemble the rodent. Hey presto – one good-as-new mouse and no sticking cursor.

You may also care to spray or wipe the keyboard and mouse with an anti-bacterial solution to prevent any risk of cross-infection. Some microbacteria survive longer than others away from the human body but there is a risk (largely theoretical, it should be said) that hardware could harbour a bug long enough to pass from one hand to another and, potentially, into the bloodstream through an open cut.

Peripherals

Peripheral devices come in so many shapes and sizes that it's impossible to generalise. However, it's safe to clean a scanner's glass plate in the same way as a monitor screen (although, being under cover for most of its life, it's likely to need little more than a dusting). Compressed air can also help blast away gunk from a printer's recesses. Most open up in one way or another, at least to provide access to the ink cartridge or toner areas, so do clean where you can. As always, read the manual for specific guidance.

Under the covers

Your computer's ventilation fan sucks air into the case but also, unfortunately, anything that happens to be floating around at the time. Most systems benefit from an internal spring clean once or twice a year, but – and it's a big but – you have to be careful. A domestic vacuum cleaner is expressly *not* suited to the job, and even a hand-held battery-powered version must be handled with care. One stray bump could mean a hefty repair bill.

As always, take safety precautions (see p.31) before lifting the lid and don't fry anything with static electricity. Now survey the scene. Are your expansion cards thick with dust? If so, there's an increased risk of short-circuits. Blast away the dust with a can of compressed air or *very* gently suck it up with a vacuum. *Don't* blow, as even the tiniest drop of saliva on your breath could cause a short-circuit. And don't follow the example of the well-meaning but dim owner who cleaned her computer's innards with lashings of hot, soapy water.

Check the cooling fan or heatsink unit protecting the processor and carefully free it of any obstructions. Also check and clean the main ventilation fan and any secondary fans elsewhere in the case. If you're feeling bold, you might even remove the expansion cards one by one, gently wipe their connecting surfaces and blast away any accumulated dust from the slots.

Don't try this at home

Never attempt to dismantle your monitor! You'll merely invalidate the warranty and it will never work again

Don't eat, drink or smoke near your PC unless you're prepared to wipe up the inevitable spillages, de-crumb the keyboard and otherwise clean up after yourself on a regular basis.

Always remember that water and electricity don't mix. Allow hardware to dry completely after even the quickest wipe from a damp cloth before switching it back on.

And if you really can't be bothered with any of this palaver right now, don't worry. When your once-beige PC turns grey, your monitor display is impenetrable to the naked eye, and your printer's pictures take on a sandy quality from all the accumulated dust within the device, we'll see you sporting those rubber gloves yet.

Treat all glass in the same way – with great care!

Expansion cards will thank you for a puff of compressed air.

PART **8** # Trouble-shooting

Although it's certainly true that your computer system is on a fast-track to obsolescence almost as soon as you get it home from the store, the good news is that hardware reliability these days is generally very high. Today's inkjet printer should still be technically capable of churning out full colour pages long after the manufacturer stops making the ink cartridges it requires. Also, most problems are evident immediately rather than, say, six months down the line. A new processor either works or it doesn't work: it doesn't *sort of* work. (For just this reason, incidentally, an expensive extended warranty is usually a waste of money.) You may be lucky and never experience a hardware problem; then again, your shiny new PC may be dead on arrival. Here we look at how to begin the trouble-shooting process.

PART

Trouble-shooting in general

The first and entirely natural reaction to a computer problem is often one of panic, compounded by the realisation that we haven't been quite as rigorous with our backing up regime as we might have been. What happens if it never works again? Have all our files and documents disappeared forever? It's at such moments that we wish we had a) taken a college course in advanced computing; and b) never become so reliant upon the infernal contraption in the first place.

Checklist

But just relax. Put the kettle on. Go for a walk or sleep on it. Then calmly, rationally and logically think through the problem. Here are six simple steps that just might resolve your woes:

1 Are your PC and all its peripherals plugged in and switched on? How about any switches on the cases – could these have been inadvertently knocked to the off position? Be sure to check the power supply too – could a fuse have blown somewhere, either in the main fuse box or in the device's own plug? Perhaps your surge protector has given up the ghost and cut the power as a safety precaution? Many a call to technical support – and a resulting red face – could have been spared by these simplest of all checks.

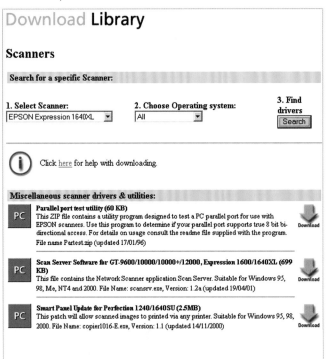

Updated drivers can cure many known problems so check the manufacturer's website.

2 Check that all cables are in place. It may mean crawling around behind your system but it's not uncommon for a USB cable to fall out of its socket and render a device inoperative.

3 When did your PC or the suspect peripheral last work without trouble? Can you undo any changes that you've made in the meantime? Hardware conflicts (see Techie Corner on p.147) are common and temporarily uninstalling a newly connected component can often fix a problem or at least pinpoint its probable cause. Poorly written software applications are also notorious for thoroughly confounding the most carefully arranged system settings.

4 If you're running Windows Millennium Edition, try the System Restore utility. This is a way of reverting the computer's configuration settings to an earlier, less problematic time.
Click Start
Click Programs
Click Accessories
Click System Tools
Click System Restore.
   Now check to see when Windows made its last 'checkpoint' and let it undo any system changes between then and now. Don't worry about your files and documents: these are unaffected by System Restore. If you're lucky, problem solved: all you have to do is work out what you did in the interim to cause all the bother. If not, try an earlier checkpoint.
   Incidentally, it's well worth using System Restore to make your own checkpoints before installing new software or adding hardware, just in case you want to reverse the changes in a hurry.

System Restore can take you back in time to a point before your troubles began.

5 Don't forget to read the manual! There's no better place to find device-specific help, and you'd be surprised at just how many potential problems are unique to one particular peripheral. In these cost-conscious days, chances are that the full manual (as opposed to that wafer thin 'quick installation guide' that fell out of the box) is an electronic file rather than a proper printed affair. It may have been installed on your PC when you first loaded the software or you may have to find it on the installation CD-ROM.

6 Finally, if your PC is working and you have an internet connection, pay a visit to the manufacturer's website. Quite possibly, the fault that you're currently experiencing is well known and a cure is already on hand in the form of a downloadable software 'patch' or bug-fixer. You'd think they'd tell you about this, would you not, especially if you registered your product when you first acquired it, but we've lost track and count of important – even essential – bug fixes slipped quietly onto support websites without any fanfare whatsoever.

Trouble-shooting specific problems

It's obviously beyond this manual's scope to cover every hardware eventuality. Indeed, it's beyond the scope of *any* manual, even those daunting 1,000+ page tomes that claim to teach you how to build a PC from scratch (but not necessarily how to switch it on). However, here are a handful of the more common problems to afflict the average computer system.

Hard disk

Insufficient disk space If Windows tells you that there's insufficient disk space to complete an operation or to save a file, you need to clear out some clutter sharpish. See p.114 for tips on uninstalling old software and making more space. Better still, pre-empt the problem now. Click My Computer, right-click on C: drive, and select Properties. If the disk is more than 75% full, it's time to start making economies.

Permanently busy If your hard disk appears to be permanently busy (lots of whirring noise and a constantly blinking light on the PC's case), chances are you don't have enough system memory and Windows is using the disk as a RAM substitute. Add more memory (see p.36).

Unexpected disk noises may be a sign of impending failure. Backup your work onto removable media (recordable CDs, Zip disks, a tape drive or similar) immediately *before* switching off your PC, and seek professional advice.

Optical drives

Disc won't eject? Restart the PC and try again. If the tray still won't open, *switch off the power*, flatten out a paperclip and poke it into the small hole on the drive's case to release the mechanism.

Problem CDs If one particular CD won't work properly, perhaps sticking during playback or freezing the system, try cleaning it with a soft cloth. If it's scratched, it's probably irreparable, although it's certainly worth trying to run it in somebody else's computer before giving up hope. If, however, you start experiencing problems with many or all your CDs, the drive itself has a problem. Buy a lens cleaning disc to shift internal dust.

Suddenly no sound from your audio or multimedia CDs? Check the PC's volume settings are not muted (double-click the loudspeaker icon near the clock in the Windows System Tray and/or run any sound card diagnostic software). If this doesn't work, the audio cable connecting the drive to the sound card has probably become detached. Open up the case (after taking all the usual precautions – see p.31) and reattach it.

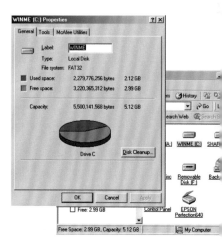

If your disk is getting full, now is the time to start making economies.

Turn to your sound card's diagnostic utilities to trouble-shoot audio problems.

Set the refresh rate as high as your graphics card and monitor will allow.

DVD disc won't play? Check that it has the same regional code as your DVD drive (see p.64). Windows itself can't play DVD movies so you need a DVD player program. Is this installed?

Monitors

Unusual patches of colour on the screen, especially near the edges, are probably due to some magnetic influence. Use the degauss button or software utility to remove excess magnetism and move any magnetic sources – including speakers and the PC case itself – further from the monitor.

Flickering If you can see any flickering in the screen image, the refresh rate is too low. This way lies headaches and a most uncomfortable user experience. See p.92 and make sure that the refresh rate is set to at least 72Hz (or higher if your monitor supports it).

TECHIE CORNER

Disk disaster
Hard disks don't go on for ever (although most are still spinning quite happily come the time for an upgrade) but, short of a catastrophe like complete destruction or theft, it's almost always possible to recover data from a badly damaged disk. Many companies worldwide specialise in data recovery, and some will even attempt a diagnosis through a modem link. The problem is that it's always an expensive option. That's why it pays to archive your old data on Zip disks or recordable CDs or similar.

However, if you simply must

recover current data, the procedure depends upon the severity of the problem. If you've accidentally deleted the odd file or reformatted an entire disk and now wish you hadn't, or if a virus wreaked havoc, specialist software alone can sometimes recover your data. In the case of physical damage, a disk that's still working from an electro-mechanical point of view – i.e. still spinning – is relatively easy to work with, but even a device badly damaged by a power surge or fire can sometimes be persuaded to yield usable data. Not one to try at home you understand: call in the experts.

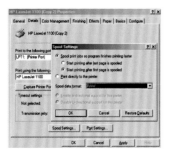

Modern printers typically have a host of configurable options.

Are paper size and layout settings correct?

Games and other software can play havoc with your display settings so go back to basics. Click Start, point to Settings, click Control Panel, and then double-click Display to access the options.

Printers

Poor print quality? This could be down to your choice of paper or some problem with the software settings. Experiment with different paper types and weights and be sure to run any diagnostic program that came with your printer. Also try printing at different resolutions.

Toner If your laser printer's toner is almost exhausted, remove the cartridges and rock it gently from side to side. This re-distributes the remaining toner and may see you through until you can buy a refill. Note that shaking an inkjet's ink cartridges does no good whatsoever.
   Inkjet cartridges can move fractionally out of the correct alignment, leading to blurred, bleeding or fuzzy prints. Run the appropriate software utility to fix this.

Blurrred Is what you see on screen most definitely *not* what you get on paper? Check that the correct paper size is selected in the print setup settings and be sure to select portrait or landscape views as appropriate.

Paper jams are less common these days than once they were but can still stop a printer dead, particularly if you use a paper type or weight that the printer is not designed to accommodate. Consult the manual for instructions on how to open the unit and extract the mangled sheets.

Modems

Connection Can you hear your modem in action as it dials up your Internet Service Provider (ISP)? Adjust the volume control on an external model until you can hear it chirruping when it tries to make a connection. For an internal modem, click Start, Settings, Control Panel, Modems and adjust the volume in the Properties section of the General tab. So long as you can hear *something*, the modem's not entirely lifeless and the problem is likely to be with the telephone line or, more commonly, a temporary hitch with the ISP.

Has your modem suddenly stopped working? If you've recently added a new extension handset or fax machine somewhere in your house, there may now be too many devices trying to share the same line. Try temporarily unplugging any additions and see if your modem comes back to life.

Diagnostics Try running the Windows diagnostic utility. Click Start, Settings, Control Panel, Modems and select the Diagnostics tab. Highlight your modem and click More Info. Windows now tries to contact the modem and reports back with any problems. 'Port already open' is the most common error message, and invariably means that some software application – perhaps a fax of voice-mail program – is messing up the settings. Close down all running programs and try again.

Pump up the volume to hear if your modem's alive or dead.

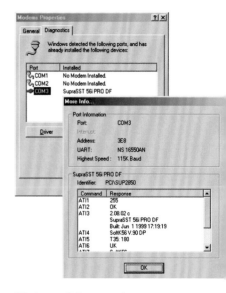

Windows will have a stab at rooting out modem troubles.

Are you connected If you *think* that you're online but can't access any websites or send and receive email, make sure that you're really connected. Click Start, click Run, type 'winipcfg' (without the quotes), and hit Enter. If you see an IP Address that's not just a string of zeroes, you are indeed online and it's likely that the problem is a blip with your ISP. If not, your modem is failing to connect. For serious diagnostics, look here (and yes, this does rather presuppose that you can get online, in which case why do you need a modem trouble-shooter?):
http://support.microsoft.com/default.aspx?scid=kb;EN-US;q142730

An IP address is a guarantee that you're online.

TECHIE CORNER

IRQ-some When hardware devices talk to the rest of the computer, they use one, more or none of the following: Interrupt Request (IRQ), Input/Output address (I/O), Direct Memory Access (DMA) and Memory Address. The first of these, IRQ, frequently leads to conflicts where two devices fight over access to the processor and system resources. Thankfully, Windows can configure most modern 'Plug-and-Play' devices (including *all* PCI expansion cards) automatically, but older ISA expansion cards may have jumpers that need to be set correctly.

In the event of a hardware conflict (warning signs: a new peripheral device or expansion card doesn't work or Windows starts freezing and/or crashing inexplicably), get along to Device Manager and look for evidence.
Click Start
Click Settings
Click Control Panel
Click System
Click the Device Manager tab.
Expand the list of hardware by clicking the + signs and look for anything marked with a (!) – an indication that Windows suspects a problem. Highlight any such devices and click Properties for details.

The most common state of affairs is when two devices try to share a single IRQ. Windows will then prompt you to (temporarily) disable one in order to use the other. This very rapidly becomes a pain, so a better solution by far is to reassign their IRQ addresses. Sounds complicated? Not really – but the precise solution depends on the specific problem. Note too that Windows can share a single IRQ address between certain devices, so just because two bits of hardware have the same IRQ doesn't necessarily mean that you need to fiddle unless one or the other doesn't work or there's a (!) warning in Device Manager.
Look here for a detailed exposition of IRQ and its system stablemates:
http://www.pcguide.com/ref/mbsys/res

Windows XP: the cure for all ills?

Microsoft's latest operating system for PCs, Windows XP, has been widely heralded as its most stable platform yet. We haven't focussed on it much in this manual simply because you are unlikely to be able to run XP on an older computer i.e. one in imminent need of upgrade or repair.

Here are the stated minimum system requirements for the Home version of XP:

Pentium II 233MHz processor

128MB RAM

1.5GB free hard disk space

However, this really is the absolute minimum that you'll get away with: XP runs a lot more smoothly with a 600MHz-plus processor and 256MB RAM under the hood.

XP comes pre-installed on (virtually) all new PCs these days but we'd hesitate to recommend it as an upgrade unless you're confident that your system can cope. Also, because XP doesn't support all older hardware, you may find that you can't get a suitable driver for your creaky printer or peripherals. Some software may also refuse to work.

For absolute peace of mind, download and run Microsoft's Upgrade Advisor, a tool that scans your PC and reports back with any potential problems. Unfortunately, it's a 50MB(!) download, which makes it impractical unless you have a high-speed broadband internet connection. You can get Upgrade Advisor here:

http://www.microsoft.com/windowsxp/home/howtobuy/upgrading/advisor.asp.

Alternatively, try the Windows Catalog tool on Microsoft's website. This lets you check your hardware and software piece by piece for XP compatibility:

http://www.microsoft.com/windowsxp/home/howtobuy/upgrading/checkcompa t.asp.

If in any doubt, follow our advice on p155 and install XP in a separate hard disk partition.

No more crash and burn

If Windows XP is indeed for you, improved reliability is the welcome result. At the simplest level, because XP is better at predicting and averting impending trouble, this means far fewer computer crashes. Wisely, XP stops dodgy third-party software from mucking up its settings in the first place and, should one

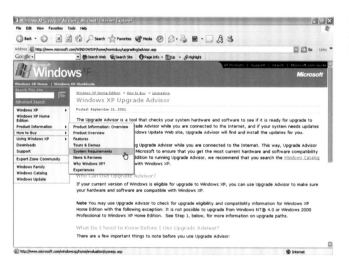

Windows XP is the best operating system around but don't consider it unless your PC is up to speed

application freeze during use, it's usually possible to close it and carry on without rebooting the computer. Like Millennium Edition, XP includes the System Restore utility which takes regular snapshots of the computer's configuration settings and lets you revert to an earlier point should anything suddenly go awry. The Help and Support centre also includes some useful step-by-step diagnostics, and there's a one-click link to the Windows Update website where you can keep your PC current with essential patches and bug fixes.

Thanks to its Windows 2000 Professional heritage, the bottom line is that XP has superior trouble-shooting tools to any other version of Windows, while being more resilient and resistant to damage in the first place.

Virtual help

But perhaps the most innovative feature in XP goes by the name of Remote Assistance. The idea is simply this: many, perhaps most, PC problems can be quite easily fixed by somebody who knows what they're doing, so why send your computer back to the store for repair when you can get instant help from a clued-up colleague, friend or family member? With Remote Assistance, you invite another XP user to access your computer remotely over the internet (or local network), whereupon they can control your mouse and keyboard and work with your PC just as if they were sitting beside you at your desk.

The system works strictly by invitation only – i.e. it's up to you to initiate the help session by inviting somebody you trust to come onboard and take control – so there's no danger of hackers breaking in, fiddling around and stealing your files. With the right help at the other end of your internet connection, the end result can and should be a computer that's up and running again in no time.

The ultimate hands-on trouble-shooter? It's certainly a welcome step in the right direction.

When all else fails, invite an expert to fix your computer over the internet with XP's Remote Assistance

Keep your computer trouble-free with automatic updates

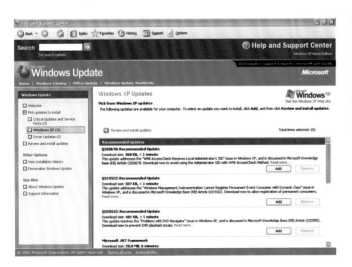

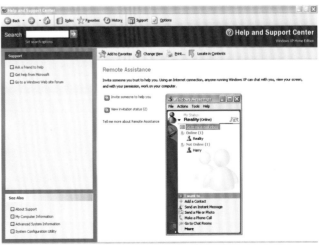

PART **9** # Appendices

PART **9** # Appendix 1
Upgrade limitations

Although it pains us to say it, there are times when it's smarter and downright cheaper to toss an ancient PC on the scrap heap (or, better, to donate it to a school or charity) and go buy a new one. In theory it's just about possible to upgrade just about everything, but computer components are largely interdependent. In practice this means that you can't, say, bolt a 30GB hard drive on to a vintage 1994 PC and expect it to work: the BIOS (see p.153) simply won't support it.

Likewise, a system running Windows 3.1 or even Windows 95 can't do a thing with USB, so a new operating system is needed before you even think about adding the like of a USB scanner. But Windows 98 needs 64MB of RAM to run efficiently (32MB at a pinch) and your old PC might have a paltry 8Mb or so onboard. In other words, a memory upgrade might be in order *before* the operating system upgrade that would enable you to add a USB controller card. And even if you do get your system up to speed, does it actually have a free PCI expansion slot? You see the problem…

The pace of hardware development is such that even comparatively modern machines are often unable to cope with an upgrade in one area unless you simultaneously improve various other key components. Say you treat yourself to a camcorder and want to use your computer for video editing. Installing a FireWire expansion card is a good first step, as this enables you to capture the footage on to your PC. But where are you going to store it? Digital film swallows up roughly one gigabyte of disk space per four minutes of footage, so you need a monolithic hard disk to make it a worthwhile exercise. On top of that, a fast processor (at least a Pentium II) and stacks of RAM are essential unless you have the patience to wait an age for every minor tweak to render on screen. Similarly, adding a DVD drive (even with a decoder card) to a first generation Pentium system isn't going to cut the mustard in the home entertainment stakes.

The bottom line is that it's important to consider the pros and cons of any potential upgrade, check whether your system meets the minimum system requirements, and be realistic about the possibilities.

PART

Appendix 2
BIOS and CMOS

Two more dread acronyms! BIOS stands for Basic Input/Output System and is usually found in the shape of a chip on the motherboard. BIOS kicks in when you first start your PC to get the essential parts of the system – keyboard, monitor, hard disk, ports and so on – up and running before (and independently of) the operating system. Modern BIOSs are Plug-and-Play, which means that they can automatically recognise and configure most new expansion cards and hardware devices. They tend also to be flash upgradable – i.e. they can be updated via an internet download.

The historical trouble with BIOS is that pre-1994 versions couldn't recognise hard disks larger than 528MB; pre-1996 versions managed no more than 2.1GB; and more recent chips gave up at 8.4GB. The good news is that special software (usually supplied with large hard disk drives) can circumvent these infuriating limitations. However, a flash upgrade or even a replacement chip is a better long-term option. If your computer was made by a major manufacturer like Compaq or Dell, you should be able to download a BIOS upgrade from the Support section of the manufacturer's website. With smaller PC brands, however, you'll have to find out who made your PC's BIOS. Look for the name during the start-up process – probably Award, Phoenix or AMI – or follow this procedure:

   Click Start
   Click Settings
   Click Control Panel
   Click System
   Click the Device Manager tab.
   Now click the Print button, select System Summary, and click OK. At the very top of the first page to be printed you'll find the BIOS details.

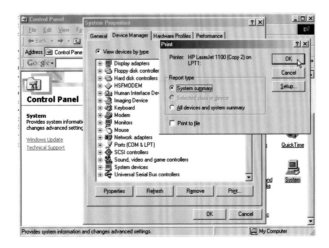

A Device Manager report reveals who made your BIOS. Check the manufacturer's website for further details.

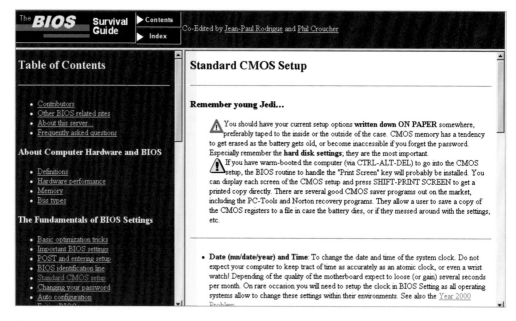

Standard CMOS Setup

Remember young Jedi...

⚠ You should have your current setup options **written down ON PAPER** somewhere, preferably taped to the inside or the outside of the case. CMOS memory has a tendency to get erased as the battery gets old, or become inaccessible if you forget the password. Especially remember the **hard disk settings**; they are the most important.

⚠ If you have warm-booted the computer (via CTRL-ALT-DEL) to go into the CMOS setup, the BIOS routine to handle the "Print Screen" key will probably be installed. You can display each screen of the CMOS setup and press SHIFT-PRINT SCREEN to get a printed copy directly. There are several good CMOS saver programs out on the market, including the PC-Tools and Norton recovery programs. They allow a user to save a copy of the CMOS registers to a file in case the battery dies, or if they messed around with the settings, etc.

- **Date (mn/date/year) and Time**: To change the date and time of the system clock. Do not expect your computer to keep tract of time as accurately as an atomic clock, or even a wrist watch! Depending of the quality of the motherboard expect to loose (or gain) several seconds per month. On rare occasion you will need to setup the clock in BIOS Setting as all operating systems allow to change these settings within their environments. See also the Year 2000 Problem.

A pencil and paper (remember them?) come in handy for making a record of CMOS settings.

CMOS means Complementary Metal-Oxide Semiconductor. This is essentially a form of permanent memory, powered by a battery, which keeps a record of your system's configuration when the power is off. Here you might change details about, for instance, the drive order in which your PC tries to boot (usually floppy drive followed by the hard disk), power management settings, port configuration and BIOS settings.

Doesn't sound like much fun, does it? Truth to tell, you might never need to go near CMOS. However, should the battery ever fail or something else go seriously awry, a permanent record of your CMOS setup would prove invaluable. Now would be a very good time indeed to make just such a document.

To access CMOS, look for onscreen instructions next time you switch on your PC (usually 'Press Del to enter Setup' or press the F2 key or similar). You'll find instructions on screen on how to navigate using the keyboard, so go to the CMOS pages and write down everything you see. Be sure to make an accurate record of all details pertaining to your computer's disk drives, especially capacity, cylinders, heads, landing zone (don't ask), sectors and anything else you can see. When you're through, press the Escape key until you're back at the start page, and confirm that you want to exit without making any changes. Windows will now start as normal.

For more on this stuff, check the excellent BIOS survival guide here: **http://burks.bton.ac.uk/burks/pcinfo/hardware/bios_sg/bios_sg.htm**

Appendix 3
Partitioning your
hard disk

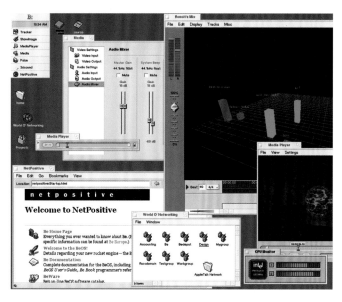

As we stated at the outset, this is a manual for PC owners, not the Mac brigade. More than this, we have been dealing exclusively with the Windows-based systems. But there are alternatives out there, notably the inexpensive Linux operating system. The problem with Linux is that it's just not suitable for non-experts. It's powerful, fast, endlessly flexible and stable – but it's a nightmare to set up and, despite a choice of bolt-on graphical interfaces, remains at heart a text-based system. See *www.linux.org* for more information.

Now, we'd be the first to encourage people to experiment with alternative operating systems but don't throw out the baby with the bath water. It makes more sense to install a second operating system alongside Windows rather than replacing one with the other, just in case you and the newcomer don't get along.

The trick lies in creating disk partitions. This process effectively splits a hard disk into two or more independent sections. Each operating system can then be installed into a different partition as though it was a physically distinct hard disk. Every time you start your computer, you simply choose which system you want to work with.

Linux can look any way you want it to. It can even look a little like Windows.

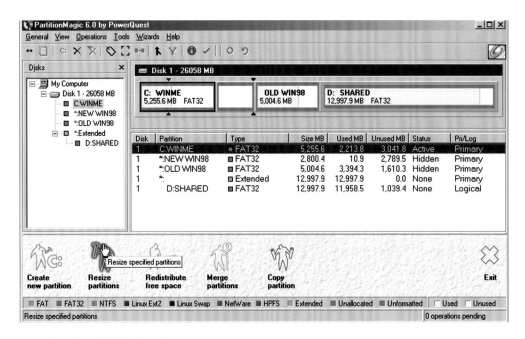

A partitioned hard disk looks and behaves for all the world like two or more distinct computers.

Disk partitioning can also help you organise your data. You might, for instance, split a large hard disk into four partitions: the first holds Windows Me; the second holds Windows XP; the third is reserved for storing files; and the fourth is used for applications and games. One advantage of storing important files on a separate partition is that they are protected from harm if and when Windows throws a wobbly. Another is that you can easily back up an entire partition and safeguard all your files at a stroke.

Windows comes with its own DOS-based partitioning utility called Fdisk. However, as Microsoft points out: "You should not use this tool unless you are very familiar with the process of partitioning a hard disk." Quite. Moreover: "When you run the **fdisk** command to create, delete, or change a partition, all of the data on that partition is permanently deleted." What this boils down is that Fdisk is fine for creating partitions on a brand-new hard disk, as we did back on p.53, or for scrubbing a disk clean and starting again from scratch – but it's not at all suitable for creating new partitions on an otherwise healthy computer.

Instead, we'd recommend using a specialist partitioning program like Partition Magic from PowerQuest (http://www.powerquest.com/partitionmagic). Even here, the process is not exactly intuitive but you can create, delete, copy, merge and otherwise manipulate partitions without loss of data. That said, you should always make a complete backup of all your important files before running any partitioning software on your hard disk – just in case.

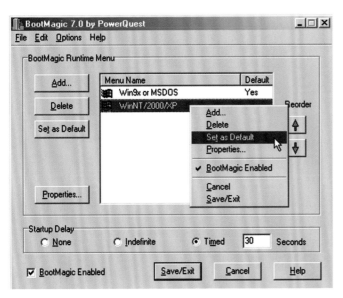

A boot manager lets you swap
between operating systems.

Make life easy with a partitioning
utility.

What you need to know

The language of partitioning is dense and confusing, and it seems that every possible action is subject to dozens of qualifiers. While utilities like Partition Magic provide wizards to simplify common tasks, it is still advisable to understand the basic principles and terminology. Here is a very potted guide to the basics.

Master Boot Record A vital file that tells your computer where on the hard disk to find the operating system. Without this record, it would be unable to start, or boot. The MBR also includes details of any disk partitions.

Boot manager A program that lets you swap between partitions in order to run multiple operating systems on one computer. A good boot manager kicks in every time you restart and offers a choice; less flexible versions must be configured from within Windows before closing down .

File system The File Allocation Table, or FAT, is a record of every file's location on the hard disk. This in turn depends upon the rules of the file system. As disks have grown in size, file systems have adapted and improved, and newer operating systems are designed to take advantage of these developments. The main file systems for Windows are as follows:

File system	Appropriate for
FAT	Windows 95a
FAT32	Windows 95b; Windows 98; Windows Millennium Edition; Windows 2000; Windows XP
NTFS (New Technology File System)	Windows 2000 (recommended); Windows XP (recommended)

You choose which file system to use whenever you create a new partition. Note that Windows 98 and Me can not 'see' NTFS partitions, whereas 2000 and XP are backwards-compatible with FAT32. In the example we gave above, you should use the FAT32 system for the data-only partitions to ensure that you can access your files and applications from within either Me or XP.

Partition types Ancient computer wisdom decreed that any hard disk may have a maximum of four partitions. These are called the 'primary' partitions, and you can install a separate operating system on each. However, it's possible to cheat by turning a primary into an 'extended' partition, which may itself be split into several 'logical' partitions. The really important point is that only primary partitions are bootable, so logical partitions are suitable for files and applications but not operating systems.

PART  8

Appendix 4 Guide to connectors

Too many holes and don't know how to fill them?
Here's a quick guide to common computer connectors.

PS2 ports and plugs.

Name	Connects what?
PS/2	Mouse and keyboard
Serial	Mouse (old-style), modem or handheld electronic PDA/organiser
Parallel	Printer and sometimes a scanner
USB (Universal Serial Bus)	Pretty much all new peripherals that once used the slower serial or parallel connectors
FireWire (or IEEE 1394)	External drives. Also ideal for connecting digital camcorders
VGA (Video Graphics Array)	Monitor
RJ-11	Modem to the telephone line
RJ-45 (Ethernet)	Computer to a network
3.5mm	Speakers and microphone

Serial port and plug.

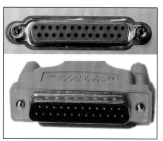

Parallel port and plug.

USB ports and plug.

Firewire port and plug.

VGA port and plug.

RJ-11 port and plug.

RJ-45 port and plug.

3.5mm ports and plug.

PART 8

Appendix 5 Building your own PC

Well, why not? We hope that by now you will have seen how straightforward upgrading a computer can be. Putting one together from the ground up is every bit as easy, and has three clear and (nearly) compelling advantages over buying a system sold on the high street:

- **It's cheaper**

In fairness, this rather depends upon how you shop. If you visit computer fairs or use mail order or internet outlets, you should be able to pick up some real bargains and easily undercut the price of a similarly specified off-the-shelf system.

- **It's tailor-made**

By designing and building a computer that precisely meets your needs, you can avoid the rip-off bundles that inflate high-street prices in the guise of added value. (Free digital camera! Free scanner!! £1,000s of free software!!! – you know the kind of thing.)

- **It's satisfying**

It really is. At the risk of sounding unpardonably geeky, there's nothing quite like the buzz of powering up a home-built PC for the first time and discovering – to your surprise, perhaps – that it works.

The golden rule of DIY computing is simply this: do your research and compile a precise shopping list before you start. If, say, you have an old but reusable sound card that requires an ISA slot, be sure to buy an ISA-enabled motherboard (not so common these days). Would you settle for graphics built in to the motherboard or do you need more powerful AGP visuals? Are you confident enough to buy your processor, motherboard and cooling mechanism separately or would you be happier knowing for sure that they will work together? In the example that follows, we made life easy by using an Intel motherboard designed specifically for an Intel Pentium 4 processor. Moreover, we made sure that the processor was boxed with a compatible heatsink/fan unit.

Oh, the other golden rule is to keep the manuals that come with your components. You'll be needing them.

Choose your components with care.

You can save big money at a computer fair – if you know what to look for.

Mid-range P4 processors are now something of a bargain.

Installing the motherboard and processor

In this example, our starting point is an ATX (i.e. full-sized) tower case. Although perhaps larger than you might like if space is tight, the ATX design is spacious enough to offer plenty of working room and lots of scope for future upgrades. It also offers flexibility over your choice of motherboard, since ATX, AT and Baby AT boards should all fit.

One tip at the outset: buy a case with a power supply pre-installed. Although you can buy a power supply separately, there's always the possibility that it won't fit inside your case or that you'll have trouble persuading the cooling fan to work. It's just more to worry about. Another tip: don't settle for less than a 300W unit. If you install a full complement of drives and a powerful processor, a 250W supply may struggle to keep up with demand.

Set up your workspace with care, ensuring that you have adequate light, space and – vitally – time. This entire process should take less than an hour but you really don't want to be starting and stopping unnecessarily. Refer to the manual if you can't figure out how to open the case – not always as easy as you might suppose – and remove the side covers.

Important: Static electricity kills all known motherboards dead! Re-read pages 30 and 31 and get yourself an anti-static wrist-strap now if you don't already have one.

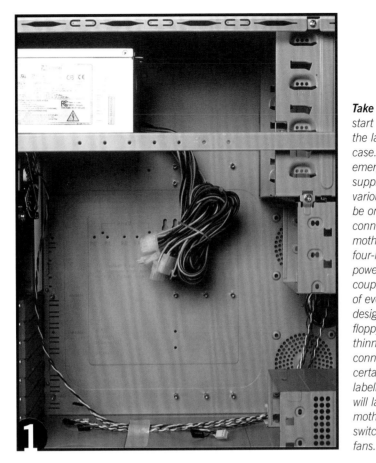

Take a little time before you start to familiarise yourself with the layout of your computer case. Note the cluster of cables emerging from the power supply and identify all the various connectors. There will be one large rectangular connector for powering the motherboard, several smaller four-hole connectors for powering internal drives, and a couple
of even smaller connectors designed specifically for the floppy drive(s). Also note the thinner wires with tiny connectors. These will (or certainly should) be clearly labelled by function and will later connect to the motherboard to power lights, switches, a speaker and cooling fans.

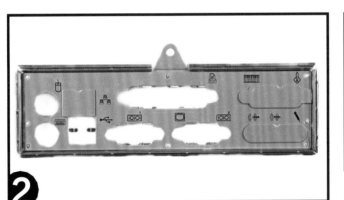

Your motherboard has an array of input and output connectors, by which means the keyboard, mouse, printer, USB and other devices will be connected. On the back of the case, just below the power supply unit, you will find an input/output shield, or plate, with spaces for all these

connections. Unfortunately, motherboard designs vary so the holes may not be in all the right places. If a shield was supplied with your motherboard, align it with the plate on the case and ensure that it matches exactly. If not, simply replace one with the other.

The motherboard will be supported on an array of brass, copper or plastic stands. These might already be fitted but you may be required to screw or snap some or all into place. As always, check the manual for details: some holes in the case will be intended for an ATX-sized motherboard but others may be for smaller AT or Baby AT designs.

4 **Carefully** remove the motherboard from its anti-static bag, hold it by the edges, and position it inside the case. Be sure to align the array of inputs and outputs with the shield described above. All the connectors should now be accessible from the outside. Consult the motherboard's manual for the location of the mounting holes, and then carefully screw the motherboard into place. Do not over-tighten the screws – doing so may crack the motherboard.

5 **What** happens next depends upon the make and design of your motherboard. In this case, it has a 478-pin socket designed for a Pentium 4 processor. However, before installing the processor itself, a base must be fitted for the cooling heatsink/fan unit. This attaches by means of four pushpins. Align these with the appropriate holes in the motherboard and snap into place. This will require some pressure but it is important that the base sits snugly on the motherboard.

6 **Examine** the socket and you will see that the corner adjacent to the lever is missing two pin-holes. Now check the pin array on the underside of the processor itself and note which corner has an identical arrangement. This is to ensure that the processor is installed correctly. Lift the processor socket lever into the near-vertical position, align the processor's pins with the socket's holes, and carefully – very carefully – position the processor in the socket. No pressure should be required to complete this operation: simply drop the processor into place.

7 **When** you are confident that the processor is seated securely in its socket with no gaps around the edges, lower the lever to lock it into place. Other types of processor sit in slots rather than sockets but in all cases installation is easy.

8 **Now** attach the heatsink. This slots into the base we installed earlier and locks into place with a pair of levers. Again, designs vary. Some heatsinks require a squirt of thermally activated glue to ensure a close bond with the processor – this will be supplied in a syringe – but here the adhesive had already been applied to the heatsink base.

 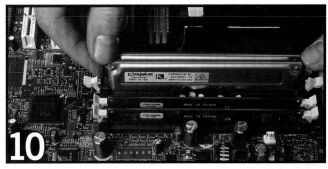

Locate the appropriate connector on the motherboard for the heatsink fan – again, check the manual – and plug it in. An uncooled processor will run for a while but will eventually self-destruct, so do this now in case you forget later.

Finally, add some memory. The full instructions for installing RAM are on p.38. In this example, we're working with RAMBUS memory where modules must be installed in equal pairs and all vacant RIMM slots filled with blank 'Continuity' modules (known as C-RIMMS).

Odd though it may seem with such a fledgling computer, you can now start it up. Connect the power supply, case fan(s) and other wires to the motherboard, and plug the PC into the mains with the power cord. If the power supply has an external on/off switch around the back, turn it to the on position first and then press the main power button on the front of the case. You obviously haven't installed a hard disk at this stage, nor a graphics or sound card, nor even a keyboard or mouse, but you can at least check that the case and heatsink cooling fans are working and that the external lights come on. The motherboard will bleep helplessly as it searches for some hardware to play with, but that's a good sign!

Caption

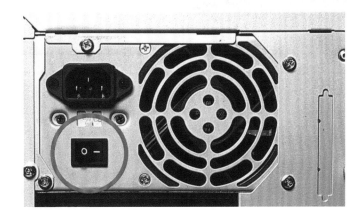

Now what?

Having assembled the heart of your computer, the rest is easy – and in fact we cover all the steps in the main body of this manual. Essentially, it's just a case of adding one component at a time, checking that it works, and proceeding with the next. Work in the following order:

If the lights come on, your DIY PC is well on the way to success.

- **Keyboard and a mouse**.

On a modern motherboard, there will be two PS/2 ports (see p.17). Plug in your keyboard and mouse, restart the PC and watch the three indicators on the keyboard (these relate to the numbers lock, capitals lock and scroll lock functions). If the lights come on, that's evidence enough that all is well.

- **Graphics card and monitor**

Again, on a modern motherboard, you'll want to use the AGP slot for top video performance (see p.72). Connect a monitor to the graphics card as soon as you install it. When you restart, you should see, well, something on screen. At the very least, your computer should show you that it now detects that it has a processor, some memory and a graphics card.

- **Hard disk drive**

Rather essential for running an operating system and storing files. Connect to the first IDE channel (see p.46)

- **Floppy disk drive**

Cheap, reliable and very helpful for starting a Window-less computer. Floppies have a special connector on the motherboard (see p.35).

- **CD-ROM (or DVD) drive**

Another essential. Connect your drive to the second IDE channel (see p.46).

- **Sound card**

It's more important to get an operating system on board than fussing with sound cards but you might as well install one now while the case is still open (see p.78).

The only half-way tricky part is installing Windows on your new hard disk. For help with this, see the section on upgrading a hard disk on p.48. With Windows at the helm, you can add a printer, modem, speakers – and, of course, application software – at will.

And that's just about that. The real trick is in the planning: source compatible, reliable components from the outset and you can't go far wrong. If you do run into difficulties, just backtrack one step at a time. The beauty of building your own computer is that for perhaps the first time you'll understand just how each piece fits into the bigger picture, and how it relates to and is reliant upon all the other pieces. With this experience and understanding behind you, you'll find it much easier to troubleshoot and solve problems in the future.

PART

Appendix 6
Glossary

Here's an at-a-glance guide to many of the techie terms used throughout this manual, along with several more that you'll doubtless come across on your travels around the mind-numbing world of computer jargon. Always remember this: if in doubt about what something means, just ask (at which point you'll invariably find that the salesperson, who is so keen to take your money, doesn't really have a clue either).

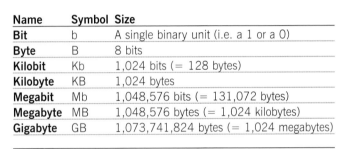

A hard disk.

Let's start with a table of the storage units used in computer-speak.

Name	Symbol	Size
Bit	b	A single binary unit (i.e. a 1 or a 0)
Byte	B	8 bits
Kilobit	Kb	1,024 bits (= 128 bytes)
Kilobyte	KB	1,024 bytes
Megabit	Mb	1,048,576 bits (= 131,072 bytes)
Megabyte	MB	1,048,576 bytes (= 1,024 kilobytes)
Gigabyte	GB	1,073,741,824 bytes (= 1,024 megabytes)

286/386/486 Early processors from Intel used to power desktop computers. Eventually superseded by the Pentium processor

56,000bps/56Kbps The theoretical top speed of modern modems (i.e. capable of receiving up to 56,000 bits of data per second)

AGP Accelerated Graphics Port. A computer interface (usually a slot on the motherboard) designed for a high-performance graphics display

Analogue A continuous signal

Anti-virus software A program designed to protect a computer from malicious viruses

ATAPI Advanced Technology Attachment Packet Interface. An interface for connecting disk drives to a computer

ADF Automatic Document Feeder. An attachment for scanners and printers that enables multiple sheets to be processed without manual intervention

Backup A copy of vital computer files made for safekeeping

Bandwidth A measure of how much data can be transferred at any one time

BIOS Basic Input/Output System. Software stored in a chip that controls the operation of a computer at its most fundamental level

A BIOS chip.

Blanking plates Removable covers on a computer case that protect unused expansion slots

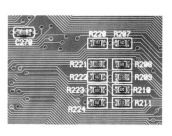

Bus A path on a motherboard through which data can pass

A motherboard bus.

CRT Cathode Ray Tube. The glass tube used to produce an image in a television set and computer monitor

CD-ROM A version of the compact disc that holds computer data. CD-R (Recordable) and CD-RW (Rewritable) formats are blank discs on which files may be saved with a CD writer driver

Celeron A slower but cheaper version of the Pentium processor

Chipset Integrated circuits on the motherboard that provide support for the microprocessor, memory and expansion slots

Clock speed The rate at which a computer's processor operates, expressed in Megahertz or Gigahertz

CMOS Complementary Metal-Oxide Semiconductor. A chip that remembers basic system settings

A CRT monitor.

Colour depth A measure of how many colours a monitor can display. 1-bit colour is black and white; 24-bit colour is up to 16.7 million distinct hues

COM port Communications port. A connector for devices like printers and modems

Control panel An area in Windows where you can configure your PC

CPU Central Processing Unit. The main system processor

Crash When the computer goes wrong and stops working!

Cursor An arrow on the screen controlled by the mouse, or an insertion point in a document

Defragment To reorganise files that have become split up and are stored piecemeal on the hard disk

Desktop The main screen within Windows before you launch any programs. The Desktop is home to icons like My Computer and the Recycle Bin

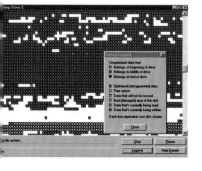

Dial-up Networking The program Windows uses to connect a computer to the internet through a phone line

Digital In contrast to analogue, a digital signal is composed of discrete packets of information (basically, a series of on/off signals)

DOS Disk Operating System. A text-based operating system for PCs developed by Microsoft. DOS was the precursor to Windows

Dot pitch The distance between the tiny dots on a monitor screen that together make up a picture

Defragmenting a hard disk.

DPI Dots Per Inch. A measure of an image's resolution. The higher the DPI, the greater the clarity

Download The process of acquiring a file on to your PC from the internet

Drive A machine that reads data from and writes data to a disk

Drive bay A space in a computer reserved for a drive

Driver A software program that lets the operating system 'talk' to and control a device

DSL Digital Subscriber Line. A technology that offers high-speed internet connections over standard copper telephone lines. The common UK version is Asymmetric DSL (ADSL), which allows more data to be downloaded than uploaded

DVD Digital Versatile Disc. A type of compact disc capable of storing a huge amount of data, including movies

DVI Digital Visual Interface. An interface used to connect digital monitors to computers

EIDE Enhanced Integrated Drive Electronics. An interface for connecting devices like the hard disk to a computer

EPP Enhanced Parallel Port. The modern, fast version of the parallel port used to connect a printer (a replacement for the slower Centronics standard)

Ethernet A technology that enables several computers to be connected together in a network

Expansion card A circuit board that can be added to a computer to enhance its capabilities

Expansion slot An interface on a motherboard used to connect an expansion card

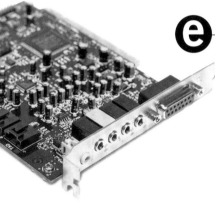

An expansion card.

Firewall A program that aims to protect a computer against unauthorised access, particularly by hackers

FireWire (also known as IEEE 1394 and i.LINK). A high-speed interface with which devices can be connected to a computer

Flatbed A type of scanner that uses a flat glass plate, much like a photocopier

Floppy disk A non-floppy plastic square that holds up to 1.44MB of data (okay, it's floppy on the *inside!*)

Format To format a disk is to make it useable in a certain type of drive

Full duplex The ability to send and receive data simultaneously

Graphics card The circuitry in a computer that controls the monitor display, usually in the form of an expansion card. Sometimes called a video card

Hard disk A magnetic disk on which may be stored a great deal of data, including a computer's operating system

Hardware The physical components that make up a computer system

Icon A small clickable image that denotes a file or application within Windows

Inkjet printer A device that squirts wet ink on to paper in order to print text and images

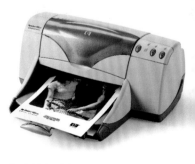

An inkjet printer.

Interface The look and feel of a software program; or the means by which computer components communicate

Jumpers on a drive.

IRQ Interrupt Request. One of the means by which hardware devices gain the processor's attention

ISA Industry Standard Architecture. The oldest type of expansion slot still found in PCs

Jaz drive A high-capacity storage device made by Iomega

Joystick A device for controlling the action in computer games

Jumpers Small pins that control the settings on drives and motherboards

Laser printer A device that uses dry toner and laser light to print text and images

LCD Liquid Crystal Display. The technology used in flat-panel monitors

MIDI Musical Instrument Digital Interface. A means of connecting electronic musical instruments to a computer

Modem A device that enables a computer to use the telephone line in order to communicate with other computers in a network, especially the internet

An external modem.

Motherboard The central circuit board in a computer to which all other devices are attached

Multimedia Loosely speaking, the combination of text, sound and video. Most CD-ROMs are multimedia, as are many websites

NIC Network Interface Card. An expansion card that enables a computer to join a network

Notebook A portable computer.
Used to be called a laptop

OEM Original Equipment Manufacturer. This refers to computer components sold directly and exclusively to manufacturers (i.e. not available to the public)

Operating system Software that governs the workings of a computer, both in terms of hardware and applications

Partition A sub-division of a hard disk that the computer treats just like a separate hard disk

PCI Peripheral Component Interconnect. An expansion slot standard, faster and more flexible than ISA

Pentium A family of powerful processors developed by Intel

Plug-and-Play A standard that enables a Windows-based PC automatically to recognise and configure any new device

Port An external socket used to connect devices to a computer

Pin 1 A method of ensuring that computer cables are connected correctly, involving colour-coding on the cable and an identifying mark on the device and connector

Plug it in and play straight away.

Processor A silicon chip that processes data. Effectively, your PC's brain

Program A set of instructions that enables a computer to perform certain tasks. One example would be a word processor

QWERTY The standard layout of the keys on a computer keyboard, where the first 6 letters on the top row are Q,W,E,R,T and Y

A RAM module.

Resolution A measure of the level of detail in an image on either a monitor screen or printed page

RAM Random Access Memory. Dynamic memory used by a PC as its working space

Registry A Windows' database with information on all hardware and software that together comprises the PC system

RF Radio Frequency. A wireless technology used to connect peripheral devices like keyboard and mice without the use of cables.

ROM Read Only Memory. As in a BIOS chip or CD-ROM, this is a form of memory used for data storage that can be accessed (read) but not changed (written)

Scanner A device that uses a light sensor to convert printed documents into data which can then be interpreted by software on a computer

SCSI Small Computer System Interface. A fast interface used to connect devices to a computer

Serial port A port on the back of a PC used to connect devices like mice and modems

Software Computer programs, including application software like a spreadsheet program and operating systems like Windows

A scanner.

Swap file An area of the hard disk used by Windows as 'virtual memory', or surrogate RAM

Taskbar A bar running along the bottom of the screen in Windows that shows which programs are running with buttons

TWAIN The software interface standard that enables scanners to work with imaging software

USB Universal Serial Bus. A relatively fast interface with which peripherals can easily connect to a computer

Upgrade To improve, enhance or modify the performance of your computer

USB connectors.

V.90/V.92 Communications standards that modern modems adhere to

VGA Video Graphics Array. A basic standard governing monitor displays (16 colours at a resolution of 640 x 480)

Video card *See graphics card*

Virus A malicious computer program, usually spread on disk or over the internet

WYSIWYG What You See Is What You Get. This means that the image you see on your monitor is exactly what comes out of your printer

Zip drive A high-capacity storage device made by Iomega

Index